ADVANCE PRAISE

"Eli is the master of SEO. His ideas have changed the game for the companies I've started and invested in. If you want to understand how to power growth with SEO, you need to learn from Eli."
—JUSTIN KAN, ENTREPRENEUR AND INVESTOR

"Bravo! Thank you so much for sharing with us your hard-won knowledge about how to drive long-term and scalable SEO results. This book is what all marketers responsible for digital growth need to understand in order to clearly communicate the 'whys,' not just the 'hows,' behind the SEO strategies to drive leadership buy-in."
—CHRISTI OLSON, DIRECTOR OF SEARCH, MICROSOFT

"Eli's fresh approach to SEO helps demystify the black box of organic search. This book is a must-read for anyone who wants to learn how to leverage this channel for growth."
—MONICA OHARA, CMO, WORDPRESS.COM

"One of the essential factors to achieving enduring market leadership is a winning, scalable distribution strategy. This book teaches entrepreneurs and marketers how to turn product-led SEO into a powerful growth engine that can build multi-billion dollar businesses."
—CHRIS YEH, CO-AUTHOR OF BLITZSCALING

"A smart, useful guide to integrated and effective search optimization. Recommended!"

—JAY BAER, AUTHOR OF *YOUTILITY*

"SEO is so much more complex than just focusing on keywords and has evolved significantly over the years. This book sets the stage for how to really manage SEO."

—LUC LEVESQUE, VICE PRESIDENT OF GROWTH, SHOPIFY

"Eli brings to the table a vast knowledge of SEO. He was able to consistently increase, year over year, SurveyMonkey's percentage of traffic from organic search. He approaches SEO holistically, in a way that works very interactively with the product and engineering team to deliver these gains with a strong consumer experience. Extremely confident this book will be a wealth of knowledge for readers."

—SELINA TOBACCOWALA, CO-FOUNDER, EVITE, GIXO

"Almost all companies create content, but if people can't find it, what's the point? Content findability is perhaps the most important part of the content-marketing process. If you read this book, getting found will never be a problem."

—JOE PULIZZI, FOUR-TIME BESTSELLING AUTHOR, INCLUDING *CONTENT INC.* AND *EPIC CONTENT MARKETING*

"In this book, Eli gives you a different view of how search engines work, what pages they want to rank, and why they work the way they do. It gives you a unique perspective of how to do SEO from many of the other books on the market."

—BARRY SCHWARTZ, EDITOR, SEARCH ENGINE ROUNDTABLE AND SEARCH ENGINE LAND

"In Product-Led SEO, industry thought leader Eli Schwartz teaches a methodology he has honed and proved 'optimizing' brands you know, iconic to upstart. In these pages, you'll learn to more clearly communicate SEO strategy to gain buy-in and align your boss, internal teams, and stakeholders."

—MARTY WEINTRAUB, FOUNDER, AIMCLEAR
INTEGRATED MARKETING AGENCY

"Eli Schwartz has mastered the art of innovative marketing as both an international leading speaker and now as an author. Eli shares his personal marketing successes. This book is clear, concise, and able to inspire by opening new ideas."

—BRETT TABKE, FOUNDER, PUBCON

"When it comes to SEO, Eli is one of the best at decoding the intricacies of the Google algorithm. This book is an invaluable resource for applying smart, data-driven insights to create lasting results for your business."

—ADA CHEN REKHI, CO-FOUNDER AND COO,
NOTEJOY; FORMER SENIOR VICE PRESIDENT
OF MARKETING, SURVEYMONKEY

"Longtime industry veteran Eli Schwartz has helped simplify the world of SEO in a way that makes it simple and straightforward for all to understand. A must-have for execs needing to know how to engage with SEO."

—ERIC ENGE, PRINCIPAL, PERFICIENT

"Whenever I need a second pair of eyes on problems related to product-led growth or scaling international SEO for any of our clients, Eli is my first call. He's the rare type of marketer who doesn't just have mastery within his discipline but can also contextualize what's actually important and will help CEOs take action."

—NIGEL STEVENS, CEO, ORGANIC GROWTH MARKETING

"Without a strategic approach toward SEO, you are leaving growth opportunities on the table. Product-Led SEO will allow you to marry your acquisition efforts with your ultimate revenue goals."
—CASEY WINTERS, CHIEF PRODUCT OFFICER, EVENTBRITE

"SEO has earned a negative reputation by focusing on tricks and hacks to fool Google's algorithm and rank at all costs. However, the best SEO marketers now realize that the best way to rank in Google is to build your product in the way that Google's algorithms optimize for. This means great content, strong engagement, and fulfilling the user's intent. Eli Schwartz lays out product-driven frameworks for how companies can build their SEO not just for quick traffic spikes, but for long-term, robust growth."
—ETHAN SMITH, CEO, GRAPHITE

"Eli's product-led method has made a huge difference in how we approach SEO prioritization and alignment across marketing, product, and engineering. He's an exceptional leader in this field— Eli has transformed the way we think about both the 'why' and 'how' of our SEO strategy, along with our growth results. This book is a must-read for any marketing, product, or engineering leader."
—ALLISON VAN HOUTEN, CHIEF MARKETING OFFICER, EPIC FOR KIDS

"Eli understands that good SEO cannot be had through a sleight of hand aimed at tricking Google into giving your site a high ranking. Instead, he relentlessly promotes the idea that good SEO comes from creating a product-led flywheel of user-valued content. That's the magic that all websites should be aiming for, and Eli has created a guide for just that in this book."
—RIDDHI SHAH, HEAD OF ORGANIC ACQUISITION, GUSTO

"Before utilizing product-led SEO, we were constantly scrambling to hit the next keyword, jump the next algorithm, and win the latest SERP. We focused on bots rather than the function of what users want and how we can help. Once I met Eli and implemented product-led SEO, the growth of our businesses and websites skyrocketed. SEO became a function to help users solve problems, not trick bots. Product-Led SEO changed my career and my company."

—JAKE GRONSKY, SENIOR SEO AND WEB GROWTH ADVISOR

"SEO is critical to building a growth flywheel, but it only works with a defined strategy. Eli's Product-Led SEO is the best guide to helping you build that strategy."

—GUILLAUME CABANE, STARTUP ADVISOR

"Eli Schwartz does a great job distilling his many years of experience leading enterprise SEO initiatives. This book isn't just useful, it's indispensable for marketers and technologists alike."

—STEPHAN SPENCER, CO-AUTHOR OF *THE ART OF SEO*; FOUNDER, NETCONCEPTS

"Especially in a world dominated by always-on mobile devices, the need for a well-rounded SEO strategy is greater than ever. Eli's ideas of product-led SEO is the exact recipe that enterprises seeking sustainable and defensible SEO should follow and build upon."

—AURELIE GUERRIERI, CHIEF MARKETING OFFICER, OPEN SYSTEMS

"Product-Led SEO is an excellent reference for product managers for a better, in-depth understanding of SEO within the product triangle, to ultimately integrate and leverage it for a successful product growth."

—ALEYDA SOLIS, INTERNATIONAL SEO CONSULTANT AND FOUNDER, ORAINTI

"SEO without a strategy is not a recipe for success. This book, Product-Led SEO, is a great primer on how to strategize, communicate, and implement SEO for long-term growth."

—GALLANT CHEN, GROWTH ADVISOR AND FORMER VP OF DIGITAL MARKETING, ZENDESK

"Product-Led SEO helps teams focus on creating content that matters and produce tangible ROI. Working with Eli over the years has given me the opportunity to learn firsthand how to blend the art of content writing and science of SEO to create a defensible business moat. Now this book shares these lessons with everyone!"

—BENNETT PORTER, BOARD MEMBER AND ADVISOR

PRODUCT-LED SEO

Product-Led
SEO

THE *WHY* BEHIND
BUILDING *YOUR* ORGANIC
GROWTH STRATEGY

ELI SCHWARTZ

HOUNDSTOOTH
PRESS

PRODUCT-LED SEO
The Why Behind Building Your Organic Growth Strategy

ISBN   978-1-5445-1957-9 *Hardcover*
       978-1-5445-1956-2 *Paperback*
       978-1-5445-1955-5 *Ebook*

I have dedicated this book to the late CEO of SurveyMonkey, Dave Goldberg. Dave was an incredible human being, and his kindness was legendary. During the time I spent at SurveyMonkey, I was a beneficiary of his immense kindness. He had a great respect for all of his employees, and he invested an extraordinary level of attention into the work I was doing.

When discussing or proposing anything related to SEO, Dave had a keen interest in learning more. He was tremendously curious. I was even able to convince him that rankings were not the goal.

Dave took an interest in my growth, and I felt like he was personally invested in my success. When I wanted to expand my career opportunities by gaining international experience, Dave took a huge bet on me just a few months before his untimely passing. Since that passing, whenever I make a career decision, the memory of Dave is with me. I feel duty-bound to make the right one.

This book would never have been possible without Dave's support. All of you dear readers are, therefore, benefiting, by proxy, from Dave. May his memory be a blessing.

CONTENTS

INTRODUCTION

"Marketing doesn't get to tell Engineering what to do." This was the response I heard from a director of engineering after making what I thought was a very basic request.

I couldn't believe my ears. It was my very first day in a brand-new job managing search engine optimization (SEO) for SurveyMonkey. I was asking for a routine technical change that anyone with my SEO background would have requested. Not only was this ask being blocked, but he'd said the sentence with a finality that suggested I would have no channel for any future requests either. This complete stonewall was an unwelcome and upsetting surprise. I'd come from a small company where I was tightly integrated with engineers open to any change that would help SEO progress. How was I supposed to do my job?

This individual was the gatekeeper for every engineering request I was ever going to make. It would be impossible for me to ever be successful if the websites could never be updated to optimize their SEO positions. I had never been a big believer in driving

SEO growth only through content; engineering relationships were critical to my SEO strategies.

Up until this momentous rejection, I had attributed my SEO successes to technical expertise: the knowledge of what changes to make and how to implement them. I suddenly realized all those years of SEO experience were worthless if the people I needed did not value my technical expertise.

Rather than throw in the towel on that day, I vowed to learn the soft skills of how to compromise with cross-functional teams and build internal political capital. By the time that engineer left the company, he had become one of the greatest advocates for SEO. He partnered with me to generate hundreds of millions of dollars in revenue from the SEO changes we made.

In writing this book, I have drawn on over a decade of experience building SEO efforts, both internally and externally, for a variety of organizations. On many occasions, I have looked back and realized my SEO success in a specific scenario was not because of what I did but how I did it. Strategic thinking was far more important than specific tactics. This book will show you how I think about many SEO topics using language that will be easily understood by internal teams to gain strategic alignment. It is my hope these ideas can help you achieve your growth goals and even further your career.

Be warned: this is not a book to teach you the nuts and bolts of SEO. There are plenty of ways to learn SEO from blogs and books, some of which are referenced in this book; rather, the goal of this book is to teach you the theory and logic behind good SEO practices. SEO is an art, and there is no rulebook. Even Google or Bing engineers who spend their days tweaking search algorithms can't predict exactly how one individual site might be visible in search. They can, however, use the principles they know to improve a website's standing, and I will teach you to do the same.

A website's visibility in a search engine is a confluence of many algorithmic rules—an infinite series of if/else code organized under the best norms of database storage and querying. Maximizing SEO visibility requires taking the known rules about search engine best practices and applying a level of creativity and logic to develop a strategic approach.

This book is written for the Marketing manager or executive who is responsible for SEO growth, whether or not they have a great understanding of the workings of SEO yet. At the same time, anyone even remotely involved in SEO should hopefully find the ideas in this book helpful in maximizing their SEO success. I intentionally do not give step-by-step guidelines. Rather, I will give you the "why" so that you, the reader, can develop your own best practices.

In this book, I put forward a theory of SEO built from over a decade of experience, something I like to think of as Product-Led SEO. The "product" is the collection of anything on your site used to draw in the user, whether those are widgets, articles, photos, apps, downloads, webinars, or really anything at all. When the goal is to get a user to click from search, it should be because something of value to them will be discovered on the other side of that click. Product-Led SEO builds a great product for users first and optimizes for search second.

Search algorithms, and even search engines, will always be changing, so a book that focuses on building search strategies to the nuances of today's search paradigms could be obsolete by the time it goes to print. However, at the core of every search algorithm, regardless of whether it is written by engineers at Google, Microsoft, Apple, Amazon, Facebook, or any other company that may one day launch a search engine, is the desire to surface search results as if they are human-curated for every specific query. Therefore, focusing on the searcher experience rather than the algorithm will be relevant until search engines cease to exist.

This book contains my best knowledge as of the time of this writing, but like everyone, I continue to learn and grow in my SEO practice. To see updated information in real time, please follow my blog at elischwartz.co. Additionally, you can subscribe to my newsletter on my site, www.elischwartz.co. I am always happy to hear from you with any questions you may have; you can email me at eli@productledseo.com.

As with all business processes, circumstances and experience will evolve our ideas over time, and we can always learn from each other. I look forward to continued conversations and feedback on your own best practices and how-tos.

I feel incredibly lucky that I have been exposed to SEO in so many different formats over the years and was able to build a career in this dynamic field. I am grateful to the managers who gave me the latitude to learn as much as I could and develop my skills.

I greatly appreciate all the clients who have allowed me the opportunity to work with them and learn from their specific journeys. I am eternally grateful to the managers in all my full-time roles who gave me the freedom to explore and learn. Most importantly, I want to thank my former team at SurveyMonkey for helping me to learn how to explain and teach SEO to others.

Most of all, I am grateful to you.

Let's get started.

CHAPTER ONE

THE BASICS OF SEO AND HOW SEARCH WORKS

For the first half of my SEO career, I lived in fear of a search engine algorithm update. I knew that my tactics were taking advantage of a loophole in a search engine's algorithm. Every time an algorithm update was rumored, I, like everyone else in the industry, quickly ran to the nearest rank-checking tool to see how I had weathered the storm.

When I joined SurveyMonkey, I had to completely pivot my approach toward the long game and be more strategic. The (slow) pace of change did not allow for me to ever take advantage of a short-term loophole. Instead of my hands shaking in anticipation after algorithm updates, I sat back and waited for the inevitable increases in traffic. Rather than lose out on traffic by search algorithms closing loopholes, I benefited, as competitors lost their visibility to my completely above-board efforts.

It was these enlightening experiences that kicked off my journey into approaching SEO with a strategic and Product-Led process. The primary goal of a search engine is and always was to benefit the user in their quest for answers. As search engine technology improves, the presentation of those answers will improve to the point where search engines may not even need to recommend any website links in response to a user's query.

Therefore, the goal of SEO is to utilize best practices shared explicitly (by guides released from the search engines) and implicitly (from historical performance data on what appears to increase visibility) to indicate to a search engine that a webpage should be relevant for certain queries. The strategic approach that I found to be most effective is Product-Led SEO. This approach reverses the traditional funnel of SEO efforts that focus on the search engine and instead focuses on the user, with the search engine acting as the medium where the product will be discovered.

When developing a Product-Led SEO strategy, planning takes precedence over individual tactics. Nonetheless, a deep understanding of tactics and best practices is crucial, as even the best-laid strategy will go to waste without effective execution.

WHAT IS SEO?

SEO is, quite simply, an acronym for Search Engine Optimization, and that is all it is. It is not a game of subterfuge with users or search crawlers; rather, it is a process of taking known rules of how search engines work and building it into a plan to improve upon the visibility you might have if you did nothing at all. There are about 1.5 billion websites in the world today, with most of them completely unaware of their SEO missteps.

Yet, search engines still have to figure out how to understand these websites without SEO, so they may get a small amount of search traffic. If that small traffic is not acceptable to you, SEO is your only answer.

To execute an SEO strategy of any type, it is important to at least have a basic understanding of how search engines work. Someday, a search engine will be as intelligent and personal as a helpful librarian, finding the exact piece of knowledge the user is seeking instantly, but that day may be far in the future. In the meantime, search algorithms are forced to rely on hundreds of factors to determine the relevance of a piece of content. Search engines also have algorithms to understand exactly what a user wants. It is the marriage of these two algorithms that results in a search page that hopefully has an answer satisfying to the user. Increasingly, the result is not even a search-results page of websites but just single answers called "knowledge boxes" or "featured snippets."

Breaking down the hundreds of factors that search engines use to understand the user's query and a webpage's relevance is what leads to the tactics and best practices commonly adopted by all SEO practitioners. Many of these factors aren't even secrets! Google, Bing, and other search engines are quite open about what constitutes a best practice. When I am asked for the best resource to learn SEO, I happily share the guides provided by the search engines themselves.

While the specifics of how to implement a tactic might be disputed, everyone—search engines and SEO practitioners alike—is in agreement that pages must contain content (not just images) that uses words closely aligned with what a user might search in a query.

SEO is simply the idea of optimizing for this reality in whatever form is necessary to improve the visibility prospects of a website. The granular details of how and where content needs to be used will vary across industry, country, and even search engine, but the question of what to put in that content is best answered by a strategic approach rather than one-off content decisions driven by narrow SEO goals.

SEO IS NOT A DARK ART (ANYMORE)

When search engines were first unleashed on the world, they were essentially online yellow pages. At the same time, early web users were infinitely more curious than yellow-page-book readers and apt to click on lots of results. Technology early-adopters quickly realized the tremendous economic windfall that could be realized from search engines sending traffic to their websites.

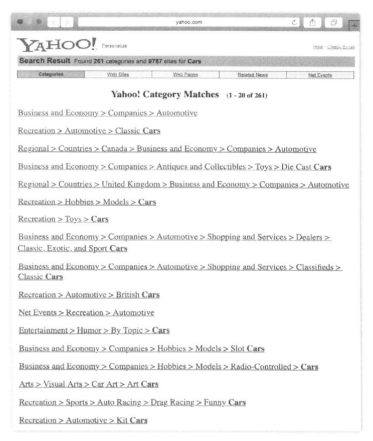

The convergence of large numbers of users and the profit potential those users represented gave birth to SEO.

At their core, the efforts behind SEO were as benign as tacking numbers and characters onto the front of a business name to appear higher in the yellow pages. However, unlike yellow-page listings, which never really engendered any emotion, early SEO earned itself a negative reputation. Many times, the people on the receiving end of these sneaky optimization strategies were regular people just trying to find an answer on the internet who were put off by seeing low-quality content and disdainful of the tactics that brought that low-quality content to them.

Originally, SEO was, in fact, a dark art. Someone looking for a vendor on a search engine could potentially land on an unscrupulous website simply because that website employed optimization tactics that allowed them to compete against legitimate vendors. In this case, the *initial* characterization of SEO is entirely fair; however, it has been more than a decade since these kinds of operators dominated the web.

Today's search landscape is dominated by Google (the actual percentages are debatable, but Google has at least 65 percent of the market share, if not more), and Google has used its vast artificial-intelligence resources to neuter illegitimate tactics that win search visibility. Initially, Google and other search engines may have been closer to software-powered phone books, but a lot has changed in the last decades. Search engines use optical character recognition to read text within images or even recognize what objects are within images. (To see the immense power of this technology, check out the Google Lens app, take a picture of something, and then search for it on Google.) Google can transcribe text within video and audio—just not at scale yet. It is already doing this for the billions of hours of video on YouTube. Most importantly, it has two decades of experience in how users respond to information and search results.

SEO today is incredibly different than it was in the early days; it is more legitimate and vastly more valuable. While many in the SEO industry perceive Google to be their nemesis, Google's aggressive efforts at fighting spam and improving its algorithms have made search a place users can trust for valuable information, which, in turn, justifies all the effort in trying to achieve success in this channel.

To really underscore this point, try to recall the last time you used a search engine other than Google or Bing and what made you only use Google or Bing to begin with. (Note: On Bing, its algorithm is similar at a high level to Google in the way it ranks websites and demotes spam.) If Google had allowed marketers to dictate what appears in search results, it might have gone the way of AltaVista, Excite, Yahoo, and all the other search engines that exist in name only while their search results are powered by Google. It is Google's quality results that make it the place users turn to whenever they have a question or need information.

SEO OF TODAY

Paralleled with the former misconception that SEO is a dark art is the idea Google and SEO practitioners are at odds with each other. This idea may have been somewhat true many years ago, but not now. Today, Google relies on SEO masters to incorporate the best practices Google needs to have the best search engine.

To be successful, SEO individuals or teams must understand what search engines look for in websites. Then, they must translate that knowledge into recommendations for product managers and engineers creating web interfaces. The fruits of those efforts will then be discovered and indexed by search crawlers and accessed by users via search engines.

Without the conduit of good SEO practitioners, Google would have to work much harder to index a web that is not in line with the way it crawls. To that end, Google works closely with webmasters. It uses its Google Search Central blog (formerly known as Webmaster Central) to share updates and conduct webmaster hangouts to answer questions. It has even started having day-long conferences for the SEO community.

As an example, Google has repeatedly said for years that it crawls JavaScript. However, it also wink-nods at the SEO community that it may not yet *crawl* JavaScript as efficiently as it would like. As a result, SEO practitioners have done Google the favor of steering web designers and product managers away from pure JavaScript websites. The collaboration allows for much of the web to be produced in a way that allows Google to index it efficiently.

THE VALUE OF SEO

The collective value of all organic traffic in the world is more than a trillion dollars. This opportunity cannot and should not be neglected. Organic is one of the only ways to generate consistent, free web traffic for many websites and products, short of building a massive brand that drives direct traffic. Building a brand is prohibitively expensive and may never be profitable. Organic search efforts, on the other hand, are significantly less costly than any other acquisition channel. They make sense.

However, Google is not going to automatically start sending boatloads of free traffic to a website just because it exists. The website needs to be constructed in a way that will most effectively maximize visibility in organic search. Without good SEO methodology, a site just relies on dumb luck to drive traffic.

SEO IN THE FUTURE

Early in the history of search and SEO, it was somewhat easy to "game" search with creative strategies or budgets, but artificial intelligence (AI) and better search algorithms have negated these tactics. Google's and other search engine's algorithms continue to improve every year toward the ultimate goal of ranking the web as a human might. This means the loopholes and hacks that are a feature of software-driven ranking will continue to close as Google and search engines, in general, become smarter.

Complaints that SEO is only getting harder are a byproduct of all the AI already included in the algorithm. Involving more AI in the search-ranking process will make optimization even harder. But why would a website surrender its future revenues to Google's AI? We need humans to understand how the algorithm works and try to put effort into getting the traffic.

Search is very much a zero-sum game, meaning if one site gets the click, inevitably, another site can't. As long as people continue to use search engines to find information, there will be a need for SEO efforts. Someone needs to be in the middle to translate the search engine's desired state into an accessible and coherent SEO effort for a given website.

Thus, SEO will never cease to exist; rather, the efforts that make up SEO will change.

KEYWORDS AND SEO

For the last twenty years, keywords have been the most important element in all search efforts. In short, keywords are the words users type into search engines. Then, the search engine matches those words with results.

In the nascent days of search technology, search engines took keywords quite literally and would return results that matched the spelling, phrasing, order, and words of a query.

The idea of keywords being the lifeblood of search marketing gave birth to an entire industry of keyword-research tools to help webmasters figure out which words are the terms most searched by users. Webmasters would then use these exact terms in their search-marketing efforts.

In the really, really early days of the internet and search, that exact keyword match was based on the meta keywords in the head of each webpage. Search engines were able to categorize and rank pages with just those words and then return results that matched.

Obviously, as webmasters figured out they could merely toss whatever keywords they wanted into the meta keywords tag, search results became pretty terrible.

Search engines then innovated on their matching technology to try to understand the actual webpage and parse out words that matched users' searched keywords. Initially, the search engines keyed in on some more important elements of the page, like title tags, headlines, and even the anchor text used in internal links.

Again, the search engine matching turned out not to be ideal because webmasters were able to sculpt results by buying links using specific anchor text, putting keywords that were highly searched into title tags, and making headlines that matched those keywords.

To address these specific search engine problems, Google had two major algorithm updates.

The first update was called Panda and rolled out in 2010. The goal of Panda was to flush out sites that used keyword matching just to rank on highly searched terms without providing content of any value to those keywords on the page. (Note: This algorithm did a lot more than just flush-out this problem; I am oversimplifying here.)

The second algorithm update was called Penguin and was released in 2012. Penguin's target was manipulative link-building practices. When Google discovered unnatural links, it levied a penalty on the site. Losing the ability to easily manipulate links took away a common tool that websites had been using to artificially boost their rankings on keywords.

Search engines, and notably Google, continued to improve on the ability to better match users with web results, and they did this on both sides of the search equation. First, Google continued to make progress in understanding webpages by looking at sentiment, word constructs, and entities within a page. Google is now better able to see when a website should be a match to a specific keyword.

On the second front, Google has made progress in leaps and bounds in understanding exactly what the user wants. Initially, search engineers focused primarily on the indexing of results to better match specific keywords in the database. The same technology of indexing results is used to get even better at understanding the user's query.

Anyone who has ever experienced fat-finger syndrome and mistyped a search has surely seen a "did you mean," where Google suggests a better spelling. Understanding a user's query is "did you mean," only it's on steroids. Google uses everything at its disposal to break down a query and really get at what the user is seeking.

Google has location data, time of day, and past search-history information, and now, machine learning is applied to the query experiences. Every bit of technology is deployed to help Google suggest the right query for the user's search. Machine learning is also utilized in the backend to search the index as if the user had typed a specific query.

What this matching means is Google is not searching out the intent of the query itself; it is changing the query that the user has written into another query with other words.

This idea of intent matching changes everything about search marketing. There is no longer an easy way to force the ranking of a keyword, which used to be possible. We now see that either the content matches the user's intent or it does not. There are many instances where Google determines the intent behind a query to be something different than what we might have expected, and there is nothing anyone can do to change the keywords back.

A new innovation, update, or development in this field could also mean keyword research is no longer as useful as it once was—and that keywords are going to continue to become even more individualized. A tool that organizes keywords by topic and intent will be far more useful.

Regardless of how things turn out, users will win—the user experience is the most important factor at present, and that is good for everyone.

HOW GOOGLE WORKS

When people refer to Google's process of ranking websites in search results, they refer to it as the "Google Algorithm." But what is that? The Oxford English Dictionary defines algorithm as "a process or set of rules to be followed in calculations or other problem-solving operations." Since Google is obviously not curated by a human, the results are driven by its software containing "algorithmic" instructions on how to understand what a user might be looking for.

There are hundreds of articles on the internet that claim to explain how Google's algorithm works. The most glaring flaw in many of these is that there is no single algorithm. Google's search ranking is a collection of many algorithms. Even Google's explanation on how search works refers to algorithms in the plural.

> These ranking systems are made up of not one, but a whole series of algorithms. To give you the most useful information, Search algorithms look at many factors, including the words of your query, relevance and usability of pages, expertise of sources, and your location and settings. The weight applied to each factor varies depending on the nature of your query—for example, the freshness of the content plays a bigger role in answering queries about current news topics than it does about dictionary definitions.[1]

In other words, trying to wrap an understanding of how Google works into one simplistic algorithm ignores the nuances of how complex search rankings really are.

---

[1]   Google, "How Search Algorithms Work," last accessed March 14, 2021, https://www.google.com/search/howsearchworks/algorithms/.

THE THREE MOST IMPORTANT GOOGLE ALGORITHMS

On multiple occasions, Google has said there are three primary algorithms that feed its rankings, each of which serves a different purpose.

1. Discovery

Discovery is the algorithm that crawls the web to identify new pages and sites that Google has not previously indexed.

The discovery algorithm is fairly robust in the tools it uses to discover new URLs. It draws on many different sources, including naked URLs (links that are just pasted into text without being clickable), XML sitemaps, Chrome, Google Analytics, and, of course, URLs submitted to Google in Google's Search Console.

The discovery algorithm simply looks for URLs and matches them against known URLs. When it finds a new URL not already on the list, it queues it for future crawling. Other than adding URLs to be crawled, discovery doesn't judge the quality of the content contained at each URL.

2. Crawling

The crawling algorithm is designed to crawl and understand the entire web.

Once a URL is discovered, Google has to decide whether it wants to expend the resources required to crawl the URL. It will use many factors to help with this decision, including the number of links pointing at the URL, where it discovered the

URL, the domain authority of the URL, and the newsworthiness of the URL.

For example, a URL it discovers from a Twitter feed with multiple mentions may get a higher score and therefore be more likely to be included in a crawl. Like the discovery algorithm, this algorithm has a single purpose. It will only crawl a page, not assess the quality of the content.

3. Indexing

The indexing algorithm determines how to cache a webpage and what database tags should be used to categorize it. This algorithm draws on library science theories as it files away pages from the internet into specific databases. For example, is a page quality medical information that is relevant for a medical search, or is it satire? Or is it news that should appear on a newsworthy query?

This is the algorithm that will determine whether the URL will be included in Google's index.

The indexing algorithm is the most complex of the three. It will decide if the content is too similar to another URL it discovered on the internet, if the website is spam or otherwise harmful, or if its quality does not meet the bar for indexation because the content might be too thin or have too many ads.

When a URL is determined to be too similar to another URL (duplicate or near-duplicate), Google will decide which URL is a better fit for indexation. The indexing algorithm will decide whether to trust the content or not based on technical SEO signals on the page.

4. Finally, the Ranking Algorithm

Ranking uses the information from the first three algorithms to apply a ranking methodology to every page. Once Google has accepted a URL into its index, it utilizes traditional library science to categorize the page for future ranking. Ranking scores drive the relative positions of pages displayed on various queries. Crawling does not guarantee something will get indexed, and indexation does not necessarily mean something will get traffic and rank on search results.

According to Google, there are five primary factors that drive the ranking score.

1. The intent of the query and how it matches the intent of the content.

The intent of the query matches more than just the words on the page. Google's goal is to understand the meaning behind the words.

2. Relevance of the page to the query.

Relevance utilizes Google's taxonomy classification. Basically, Google will try to produce relevant results, with a human medical query matched with human content rather than content using similar anatomical wording about animals.

3. Quality of the content.

Google uses AI to decide whether a user will be satisfied with what they find on a page. This can include everything from assessing the content's readability to placement on the page, size of ads, and links to the page, with more authoritative links indicating higher quality.

4. Usability of the page.

Each ranking score is important, but usability is critical, as it can demote or remove your page from results altogether. Usability can demote content that has excessive advertising or poor user experience. Poor usability will remove non-mobile-friendly pages from the mobile index. Page speed is a factor, but only if it is too slow to be used on a standard connection.

5. Context and settings.

Google uses many location and time signals to best answer user queries. If the query is determined to have local intent, the ranking will show content that matches that location, even if a location was not included in the query.

Context and settings will similarly match the location settings of a user's browser and ensure it shows content in the right language. Context and settings algorithms will also show San Francisco Giants for a baseball query and New York Giants for a football query.

this is why you can lazy Search

A FIFTH ALGORITHM

Bidirectional, encoder, representation transformer

Most SEO masters also consider Google's fifth primary algorithm, which is tasked with understanding a user's query in a deeper meaning. Since Google announced its natural-language-processing tool, BERT, its ability to understand user queries in natural language has dramatically increased.

This algorithm doesn't directly impact the rankings of websites for queries; rather, it rewrites the actual queries to what Google believes the user is searching. This algorithm takes Google even further from a search engine that ranks webpages based on how it matches what a user searched and brings it closer to matching what a user really wants. To see this algorithm in action, speak a query into Google's search bar on a desktop or mobile device and watch Google parse your query in real time.

TYING IT ALL TOGETHER

There are many factors that come into play when Google decides to send traffic to a website, and the ranking score of each of these algorithms plays a strong role. Focusing only on a piece of this process—for example, only chasing backlinks or keyword stuffing—neglects the other relevant factors that help the ranking algorithm make its determinations.

A successful SEO effort will include strategies that address all the Google algorithm and ranking-score factors. We must ensure all content is discoverable, crawlable, and indexable, and the content provides an excellent user experience. Focusing efforts on technical SEO, on-page factors, or user-experience optimization alone cannot give us ideal SEO results. We must have all three.

GOOGLE ALGORITHM UPDATES

Every time there is a rumor of a Google algorithm update, a general panic ripples through the massive community of people reliant on free traffic from Google's search users. There is a collective holding of breath while the numbers are analyzed and then a sigh of relief (hopefully) when they survive the algorithm update unscathed. (Note: Bing and other global search engines also have algorithm updates, but since many sites get the majority of their search traffic from Google, it is Google updates that become the most newsworthy. The idea of what an algorithm update is and how one should approach it is certainly the same for all search engines that exist today and likely for all search engines that might eventually be unleashed on the world.)

After the update is released, and especially if it is confirmed by Google, a slew of articles and pundit analyses attempt to dissect what it is Google changed and how to win in the new paradigm. I believe all this angst is entirely misplaced.

The Google algorithm is made out to be some sort of mystical, secret recipe cooked up in a lab designed to simultaneously rob and reward sites at the whims of a magical, all-knowing wizard. In this outdated schema, the goal of every SEO and webmaster is to dupe this wizard and come out on the winning side of every update. This idea is rooted in a fundamental misunderstanding of what happens in a Google algorithm update—and a fundamental misunderstanding of Google.

DON'T PANIC

Google wants to ensure a pleasurable user experience for the searcher. Nothing more, nothing less. It is not a wizard, and its system is not meant to rob and reward sites arbitrarily.

Google's algorithms are extensive and complex software programs that constantly need to be updated based on real scenarios. As anomalies are found by search engineers, the variations are patched in a process similar to how bugs would be reported and fixed in any other software program. In every other company, updating a core program is merely called "a bug fix," but in search, the "fix" translates to an algorithm update that often goes unnoticed.

In any software company, there are also large product updates that happen multiple times per year. There are always changes being made to the product, some visible and others not so much. As an example, Facebook is constantly tweaking all aspects of its product. Facebook didn't just launch its newsfeed many years ago and leave it. Phone operating systems, on Android and iOS, are updated in major ways at least once per year.

Google, like any other software company, releases updates with big leaps forward to its products and services. However, in Google's case, they are called "major algorithm updates" instead of just product updates. The choice of words alone is somehow enough to induce panic attacks.

ALGORITHMS DON'T HURT

You are now armed with the knowledge of exactly what a Google algorithm update is. Is it not, then, gratifying to know there is never a reason to panic?

When Google's product managers determine there are improvements to be made in how the search product functions, they usually apply mere tweaks at the margins. The updates are designed to address flaws in how users experience search. Much like how a phone operating system leaps forward in a new update, Google's major updates make significant improvements in user experience.

IF YOU SEE A DROP IN SEARCH TRAFFIC

If a site experiences a drop in search traffic after a major algorithm update, it is rarely because the entire site was targeted. Typically, while one collection of URLs may be demoted in search rankings, other pages likely improved.

Seeing the improved pages requires taking a deep dive into Google Search Console to drill into which URLs saw drops in traffic and which others witnessed gains. While a site can certainly see a steep drop off after an update, it is usually because they had more losers than winners. Any drop is most definitely not because the algorithm punished the site.

DID YOU HAVE A DROP, OR IS THAT JUST YOUR IMPRESSION?

If you see a drop, in many cases, your site might not have even lost real traffic; often, the losses represent only lost impressions already not converting into clicks. With a recent update, Google removed the organic listing of sites that had a featured snippet ranking. I saw steep drops in impressions, but the clicks were virtually unchanged. Gather and study your granular data for a clearer rendering of information rather than assuming the site has become a winner or loser after an update.

Websites that focus on providing an amazing and high-quality experience for users shouldn't fear algorithm updates. In fact, updates can provide the needed impetus to excel. The only websites that have something to fear are those that should not have had high search visibility in the first place because of a poor user experience. If your website provides a great experience for users, updates are actually likely to help you, as they winnow those poorer quality sites out of the running.

With a Product-Led-SEO approach, there will be pages that may lose some traffic in algorithm updates, but in aggregate, the site will typically gain traffic in most scenarios. Digging into the granular data of what changed will likely support the idea that websites do not suffer or benefit from algorithm updates;

only specific URLs do. Knowing the why behind the changes is more than half the battle.

PAST ALGORITHM UPDATES

If there is truly a case where all URLs in a website are demoted in an update, the dismal outcome is likely because the website—as a whole—had a disguised benefit from a "bug" in how Google works. Known or unknown by the business, the site was already living on borrowed time.

Websites that exploit loopholes in the way Google ranks the web should always be aware that Google will eventually close the loophole for the good of the entire internet.

In the more distant past, entire sites were, in fact, targeted by algorithm updates—but this is no longer the case. There were three main updates that targeted problematic sites.

- Panda was designed to root out low-quality content.
- Penguin demoted unnatural links.
- Medic demoted incorrect medical information and had specific use targets.

Other sites were left relatively untouched. The sites targeted were mainly exploiting loopholes, and their more-honest competitors often saw significant gains as they dropped out of search.

UPDATES ARE A FACT OF SEARCH LIFE

Google will, and should, always continuously update its algorithms. Google's primary motivation is to have an evolving product that will continue to please and retain its users.

Consider that if Google leaves its algorithm alone, it risks being overrun by spammers that take advantage of loopholes. A search function that provides too many spammy results will soon go the way of AOL, Excite, Yahoo, and every other search engine that is functionally no longer in existence. Google stays relevant by updating algorithms. Updates are a part of search life.

Instead of chasing the algorithm, every website that relies on organic search should train its focus on the user experience. The user is the ultimate customer of search. If your site serves the user, it will be immunized from algorithm updates designed to protect the search experience. There is no algorithm wizard— only SEO masters who have figured out how to apply best processes, best procedures, and actions for your website.

Algorithms and updates have only one purpose: help a user find exactly what they seek. Period. If you are helpful to the user, you have nothing to fear.

Building a successful strategy is contingent on understanding the basics of SEO, and fortunately, there are many ways to quickly get up to speed.

LEARNING SEO

Learning how to do SEO is akin to learning any Product or marketing pursuit. You can never truly become an expert, as there's always so much more to learn. Additionally, SEO is a hands-on pursuit and can't be taught in a classroom setting. It also changes over time as Google and search change, so we all must continue to learn.

Like any profession, SEO can be mastered more quickly by

someone who has a predisposition toward certain necessary skills: analytics, creativity, and curiosity. People skills are nice to have, but in reality, an SEO professional can be successful without ever coming into contact with other people.

Start learning SEO, if you have not already, by creating a website. Ideally, the website should be completely customizable from backend to frontend. But even if it's a canned website, like Wix or Weebly, there is learning to be had. With this website, Search Consoles from Google, Bing, and Google Analytics (the most popular website-tracking software) should be set up immediately on launch. This should be possible whether the website is built on a custom stack or a template copied from another website. If you are lost, there are many great videos on YouTube about how to quickly get started in Google Analytics, which will be enough for you to start tinkering with how it works.

Next, immediately start writing content. The content can be anything you feel passionate about that is interesting. Once there are a few pages of content, you can go about getting some links. There are some easy links to be had in social media profiles. Don't worry about whether the link passes SEO value or is a nofollow link (a way of signaling to Google that it is not to be trusted). Just get people (including yourself on various sites) to link to your new pages. If you know other website owners, ask them for links too.

Within a couple of weeks, Google will be crawling the site, and you can begin learning.

1. Go to Google, and do a search with "site:yourwebsite.com" (replace yourwebsite.com with your actual website name).

Make sure your website is showing up. Look at how the website appears in search results.

2. Go to Google's (search.google.com/search-console) and Bing's (bing.com/toolbox/webmaster) Search Consoles, and look at the keywords your website is getting impressions from.

3. While still on Search Console, look at the clickthrough rates of these keywords.

4. On Google Analytics, you can learn how users are using the website by looking into the demographics menus. The information provided there will include some of the following:

    A. Devices being used to visit the website.

    B. Cities/Countries of users.

    C. Pages visited.

    D. Number of page views per visit.

    E. First and last pages per visit.

With all these pieces of information, a curious and analytical person can begin to understand how search engines might work. Posit ideas, look to prove or disprove those ideas, and start iterating on your prior work.

- Write content that matches some of the keywords (called "queries") you see in Search Console.
- Improve the meta description used by Google and Bing as the snippet on search results to get more clicks.
- Generate more links to improve the overall position of the site.
- Find keywords you didn't know were of interest to users, and insert them into your content.

With this foundation in place, it's now worthwhile to look to outside experimenting to up-level your skills more formally.

EVENTS

My favorite place for learning is conferences. At conferences, you can meet other people who share best practices and act as resources to call on in the future. There is a lot you can learn from conference presentations and networking with conference speakers.

Some of my favorite conferences for SEO learning are:

Pubcon—Held every year in the fall in Las Vegas. There are also smaller events in Austin, Texas, and Fort Lauderdale, Florida.

SMX—Held in the spring in San Jose, California, and in the fall in New York, New York.

Content Marketing World— Held in the fall in Cleveland, Ohio.

There are likely also smaller events wherever you live, and you can learn a lot by getting connected. For example, Portland, Oregon, has a vibrant SEO group called SEMPDX; Dallas, Texas, has DFWSEM; and the San Francisco Bay Area has Bay Area Search.

BOOKS

There are a great many books on how SEO works, but many of them quickly become outdated if they explore specific SEO tactics. I have found the most helpful books to be those that dive into the details of search engines rather than specific SEO tactics.

The Art of SEO by Stephan Spencer, Eric Enge, and Jessie C. Stricchiola is a great book with many fascinating details on the why and how of SEO.

I'm Feeling Lucky by Google Employee Number Fifty-Nine, Douglas Edwards, is a great read on how Google became the monolith it is today.

In the Plex by Steven Levy is another great story about how Google succeeds.

BLOGS

There are blogs of every type on digital marketing, and many of them should be taken with a grain of salt, especially if they are pitching a product or service. These are the blogs that should be followed and read as frequently as possible:

Google Search Central (developers.google.com/search/blog)

Search Engine Roundtable (www.seroundtable.com)

Search Engine Land (searchengineland.com)

Search Engine Journal (www.searchenginejournal.com)

SOCIAL MEDIA

Twitter, Facebook, and LinkedIn can be great places to join groups for people interested or engaged in SEO. Within these groups, you can network and share information about best practices with each other.

I won't make recommendations of specific accounts to follow or groups to join, as these things constantly change. However, venturing out onto social platforms to learn more about SEO will remain a useful strategy no matter what the future holds.

Making connections with other practitioners will always be helpful.

Just a little bit of awareness around the basics of SEO is enough to begin the process of building profitable SEO campaigns; you don't need to be a master to start experimenting with SEO. Nevertheless, the basics will only help you with the tactical aspects of SEO. To be truly successful, the tactics need to be wrapped in a strategy to reach a specific and predefined goal.

CHAPTER TWO

WHAT IS PRODUCT-LED SEO?

A couple of years ago, I worked with a company called Drops, the 2018 Google Play app of the year. The company wanted to build the easiest website in the world on which to learn a new language. It would help users learn thirty-seven languages with a purely visual experience and be focused on vocabulary rather than grammar.

The app's explosive growth (over a million users) had been purely organic, and the team was looking to replicate this success online via SEO. From the outside, using search to build awareness of a dictionary product might have seemed like a fool's errand. (Google commandeers nearly all the above-the-fold real estate with their translate product, so getting clicks would always be difficult.) Even if competition from Google wasn't a factor, there were dozens of other dictionary sites that had been working on this exact product for many years, and Drops would have a lot of catching up to do.

However, this is the exact scenario where Product-Led SEO shines. In developing the plan for how we were going to build out the world's best website for learning a new language, we did very little keyword research.

The goal was never to win on any specific keyword (e.g., "bread" in German) but instead to win on many keywords, whatever they might be. The keywords where the site was visible had to have perfectly matching pages that provided a great user experience through the product. This was the only way the site was going to achieve its ultimate objective of gaining new language users.

To this end, the SEO effort was allocated toward developing product specs, taxonomy, cross-linking guidelines, and page design.

Rather than develop a straight dictionary product, like any other online translation library that targets one-to-one word definitions (Google included), and then jam as many keywords as possible onto the page, the Drops page was built with the user experience first. Just like the app product, the web version would focus on making learning easy. Extra words just for the sake of SEO would confuse the user.

Keyword research wasn't the only SEO effort ignored in this process; at no time during the SEO build process was there ever a discussion on building backlinks to the new product. Drops certainly acquired backlinks to the site, but these were simply the byproducts of building a great product and not something it proactively sought.

With these facts as the background, the outcome was astounding and underscores just how effective a Product-Led SEO strategy can be.

The website languagedrops.com had been on the internet for a few years, but up until the launch of the dictionary product in June of 2019, it received between 100 and 200 branded clicks per day from search. The largest spike had been at the end of 2018, on the day Google awarded App of the Year to Drops. Post-launch, the number of branded organic clicks remained roughly the same.

The real magic was on the non-branded search, which is where all SEO efforts should always be focused. Branded search will only grow as fast as a brand grows (a function of PR and user growth), while non-branded can have infinite potential. Prior to the product launch, the site only received a few dozen organic clicks per day. Even after the launch, it only ticked up slightly. In raw percentages, traffic had doubled, but going from twenty-five to fifty organic clicks is not very exciting.

Many founders or executives who have just invested a significant sum of money into SEO panic if they are expecting thousands of visits on day one, but SEO requires patience. By August—two months after launch—the daily clicks were up to 200 per day. Still not exciting, but ten times what the base had been just two months earlier.

Then, the magic of compounding SEO traffic began to kick in in a huge way. SEO compounds as more pages are discovered by Google and additional queries earn visibility in Google's search results. Just like compounding in an investment account, the visits get added to the base, and the growth happens on top of the principal.

Even more exciting, the impression growth that Drops began generating on search results was stratospheric. Just over a year after the SEO strategy was implemented, the website was generating nearly 30 million monthly impressions on Google, with a very healthy click-through rate on those impressions.

It should be noted that keyword research wouldn't have led us to this result. Some of the top queries driving clicks and impressions today, according to the popular keyword tools, supposedly should not have any search volume.

One final advantage to the Product-Led SEO strategy that Drops employed is that with the focus on the user and the product, it built a competitive moat. Whereas competitors might have to pivot if Google makes a monumental change in how it indexes sites, a product-led strategy would only need to change if user intent changes. While other dictionary sites are chasing the Google algorithm, Drops is chasing the user. Even if Google ceases to exist, those users will still seek out the brand that gave them exactly what they needed.

Had Drops employed a traditional SEO strategy, it would have poured all its efforts into popular keywords and would still be clawing its way ahead of competitors. Instead, its Product-Led SEO strategy allowed it to focus on all keywords—in all languages—in a programmatic and scaled process.

A Product-Led SEO effort isn't something that only works with specific companies; rather, it is a process that every website working on SEO should employ.

PRODUCT-LED SEO

Within the technology industry, and especially in Silicon Valley, there is the idea of "product-led growth," which upends the whole premise of marketing the product to promote adoption. Instead, the shift focuses on getting a great product into the hands of users who get excited enough to then become marketing agents on the product's behalf. In this paradigm, there may also be innate triggers within the product that encourage sharing, thereby forcing the hand of the user.

Notable recent examples of companies that were incredibly successful at the "share paradigm" are Slack, Dropbox, and Zoom, which become more useful for each user as the program is adopted within a larger group. Building a viral loop where the customers drive acquisition is the holy grail of any product or service. Each of these companies deprioritized traditional marketing and instead focused on building an amazing product that users would just have to share with their networks. Each of these companies grew exponentially without spending any substantial funds on early marketing.

When product-led growth is successful, a company will have acquired a large segment of users to learn from, making it easy to build marketing strategies around these users. The company can learn what caused the product to be adopted by other users or teams within a company. Given this data, it can naturally use paid marketing to encourage this adoption process on a wider scale.

I am a proponent of using the same growth approach for SEO efforts.

A KEYWORD-DRIVEN APPROACH

Too often, SEO efforts begin with just a group of keywords, a list developed by the Marketing team or founders based on their own knowledge of the product. The keywords then become the stems of keyword research. They are input into any keyword research tool, and related words are output.

The new, longer list becomes the seed for content ideas that will be written and posted on the website. The keyword list becomes a checklist and content roadmap, which doesn't change much over time. Whatever the actual performance or real-time metrics, content keeps getting cranked out using the words from the original keyword checklist.

Keyword Research

Keyword research isn't perfect. When demand is low or not yet existent for a product, the best research in the world is inadequate. Research is still forced to suffice. In this paradigm of SEO, there's no room for a user's feedback loop, and much of the content creation is all too manual.

Content intended to match keywords is written in long form, and the full library will only scale as fast as the content producers can write. The greatest gap in this approach is between the fact that the SEO strategy is laser-focused on specific keywords and an expectation of generating a high position on just those keywords.

Ranking on targeted keywords, aside from the vanity aspect, is aspirational and may never even be achieved.

Keyword-based SEO is limited and inadequate, and there is a better way.

PRODUCT-LED SEO

Instead of using SEO to market the product (when I refer to product, I am discussing the offering to the user, whether that is a service, subscription, content, or physical widget), the product should become the SEO driver. Many of the most successful websites on the internet have achieved organic dominance through this product-led approach.

Like many concepts, Product-Led SEO is more easily understood through an example than it is by speaking in generalities. Let's go through an example in depth to illustrate how Product-Led SEO can get better results in a competitive space than conventional SEO thinking.

THE TELEHEALTH EXAMPLE

Imagine for a moment, you are the Chief Marketing Officer (CMO) or Head of Product for a new company that connects consumers to doctors who can treat them via telehealth visits. Given the changing realities in how medical services are sought and offered, the company has nailed product-market fit, and demand is exploding. In addition to a heavy reliance on word-of-mouth, the company is spending hundreds of thousands of dollars per month on paid marketing to acquire new customers.

As a wise executive, you are well aware that word-of-mouth is not a sustainable strategy. (Negative word-of-mouth could quickly turn the tides of growth, and you're leaving your growth in the hands of others.) Additionally, competitors, seeing your success, are likely clipping at your heels and building their own word-of-mouth flywheels.

Paid marketing is currently very successful, but again, this is only in the short term. Eventually, the easiest-to-win customers will have been reached, and the cost of acquisition will rise. In the same vein, competitors are also going to spend as much as they can to go after the same set of users, causing costs to go up for everyone. While paid marketing might be effective today, margins will inevitably get thinner, and you will be forced to continue spending more and more to keep the business afloat.

Knowing your product is superior to the competition, you need to find a source of user acquisition that will continue to build the customer base without the need for an ever-expanding budget. In a flash of wisdom, you realize the SEO channel is driving solid user acquisition with only minimal investment.

You connect with your Digital Marketing team or external agency focused on SEO. More than likely, they come back with a proposal for an SEO audit (a topic touched on later in this book), competitive research, and a content plan mapped back to high-value search keywords.

Breaking down these proposals, you come to a sudden realization: you are not sure this proposal will lead to actual growth. The audit and competitive research will tell you exactly what you already know. The audit will tell you areas of the website that need to be improved, and the competitive research will tell you that the competition is far ahead.

The content plan also details the obvious. There are many keywords where you would like to be visible, and it will take hundreds of pieces of content to ever address all these keywords. The budget necessary to fully cover each of these words will be quite immense, especially since medical is a space that needs to have professionally vetted content, and you can't get away with an offshore freelancer.

That sneaking suspicion you had about the proposals not leading to actual growth is, in fact, correct. Many people in your position have had this hunch but, absent an alternative, they went ahead with the SEO plan presented to them. In many cases, after an investment of tens of thousands of dollars, they have a library of content that may or not be working for them; however, in all cases, it is not defensible against competition.

CONSIDERING THE OPTIONS

Your conventional SEO plan offers three underwhelming options.

First, there is the conventional keyword-optimization option. In many business verticals, keywords that drive SEO traffic are challenging, but in your health category, the problem is particularly acute. At the top of the value chain, keywords like "telehealth" or "healthcare visit" will be dominated by governments, hospitals, and potentially older competitors. Moving further down the keyword path into longer tail terms means less competition but also significantly fewer searches. This means the investment dollars will be spread even further for possibly lower returns.

Next, you might consider a local strategy. Pivoting away from these high-value terms into local would make sense for how people currently search for medical needs, but now you would be faced with competition from doctors in every single village, town, and city. To achieve dominance with this effort, you would be fighting a war with 400 fronts. Additionally, all the content needs to be manually written, which means either you would never have a page for every place, or you would end up with low-quality content—neither of which is a particularly good outcome.

There is one final option available to you in your health vertical, and that is to focus on conditions and illnesses. Again, like the other options, there is fierce competition, but this time, it is global. There are national governments, hospitals, and medical-information sites that all have something to say. Competition aside, the requirements of quality are significantly high, which means content costs might be prohibitively expensive. Some may think this is an opportunity to decrease the quality into something just a step above a glossary of definitions, but with a dictionary as the content hook, it is hard to imagine ever drawing in a potential conversion for a telehealth visit.

All of these approaches contain significant challenges, and none will result in sustainable, resilient growth.

PRODUCT-LED TELEHEALTH

Let's approach the same problem from the direction of a Product-Led SEO strategy. Rather than have SEO efforts be your marketing channel for the product, which is telehealth medicine, you are going to make the product itself be the SEO channel. This sounds like a lofty idea, but as we delve into the possibilities, it will become quite eye opening.

The goal is not to generate traffic for traffic's sake but to generate engaged users who will eventually become paying users of the product. Many keyword ideas are measured by their visible rankings on search engines, which don't necessarily translate to clicks and certainly not revenue. The idea that you should implement for SEO should be highly relevant for the user base in a way that users want to click from search, and a good number of them will convert.

The key part of building a Product-Led SEO strategy is that it is a product (an offering of any sort) that is being built. This should be approached the same way any other product is: a product plan, a roadmap, project management of inputs and collaborators, and, most of all, incorporating user feedback. Unlike a keyword-research-driven SEO effort, a Product-Led SEO strategy needs to have a product-market fit.

The best way to get to product-market fit is to learn from users and really understand what they want. Even better would be to take this user empathy and build for personas that will be the most profitable for the business.

Talking to Users

Incorporating these guidelines into your telehealth business means the first thing we are going to do is talk to our users via in-person conversations, surveys, or looking at their customer-support interactions. We are going to understand our users' pain points (no pun intended) when they seek out telehealth and what they would prefer to see online as they go through the buyer's journey of deciding to sign up for a telehealth appoint-ment. It is these pain points and desires from our current user base that we will want to extrapolate onto all our potential users by building a product that will attract them.

In our hypothetical example, we learn a few things about the user base that we had not already known. First off, we learn many people choose telehealth because of cost; they like that the cost of the visit is known upfront. Second, we learn one of the most frequent reasons people use telehealth is because of skin rashes. Third, we learn people use telehealth when they are embarrassed to go to their regular doctor. Finally, we learn people use telehealth just for reassurance that they are going to be okay but might not have actually gone into a real doctor's office for the same thing.

The First Potential Product

Now, taking everything we know about our users, we can start thinking of a product we might be able to build that would attract users with similar characteristics but at different stages in the buyer's funnel. Since we have four potential reasons people seek out telehealth, we can either combine all (or most) into one product, or we can prioritize our buying triggers based on the personas and uses that would drive the highest eventual revenue.

Now, with the buyers' motivations and sentiments in hand, we can ideate on potential product options that would match what the users might be looking for. Knowing that embarrassment, cost, and skin issues are huge motivating factors for eventually connecting with a telehealth provider, we can flip this to non-users and realize there is likely a larger population who have these concerns but never actually took the step of scheduling a telehealth visit. Some of them might have been concerned about costs, while others were too embarrassed to see a doctor they don't know on a computer screen.

Rather than create content and an SEO product designed to convince users to seek telehealth, let's instead build content and a product that appeals to those looking to avoid medical visits.

We don't have to worry that we are going to sell people away from telehealth because we are positive your business provides a valuable service if people would just know it exists.

This product could be a library of all the weirdest, most embarrassing conditions. The goal of the product would be to reassure people their problem is not that strange. They will be okay. Inevitably, there will be some people who should see a doctor, and some of your articles should recommend that. The recommendation becomes more reliable when it is not the outcome of every page but, rather, is targeted to only specific conditions that truly need a doctor. The search terms for this content would be highly varied, but you would win many of the clicks on an aggregate level because yours would be the only comprehensive library with every condition.

Let's look at some of the key aspects of this hypothetical product that we might develop and why it would be advantageous for SEO purposes. First off, this is a product designed to help all users who arrive from search. In other words, they do not need to be a paying telehealth patient. The product is monetized by those who choose to become a patient, but it is not a requirement. Second, the product is aimed at completeness—referencing all embarrassing conditions within a set category (e.g., skin conditions) and not just those with high search volume. Third, your company will choose to build this product because it does not yet exist in this form on any other website. Furthermore, you know there is demand for this product because your user research conveyed this finding to you. Fourth, and most importantly, there is a direct revenue tie-in to the core business. The content will appeal to a persona of users who you have either proven or have a strong belief will buy your product.

The Second Product Option

However, this shouldn't be the only idea you consider. You are building to a cohort of users who have many needs, and you should always consider multiple options. However, when it comes down to it, you can only pick one. Dabbling with a multiple-product strategy means you never go all in, and the whole effort has a high likelihood of failure. You will want to pick the product offering you will build based on many factors, including budget, product-market fit, ROI, and every other consideration that goes into a business decision.

Just to make sure the point about making a product choice isn't lost, let's develop another potential product idea for you, the telehealth executive, to consider. Since we know from your research that cost is a huge factor, let's try to build something that wraps medical and care costs into a single holistic product targeted at search users.

As anyone who has ever done medical-cost research online knows, there are many websites and datasets with pricing information online. However, you, in your research process, discover there is no source of data for total cost of care for any illness that includes transportation to doctor visits, hospitalizations, follow-up visits, pharmacy costs, and waiting time in a doctor's office. In a flash of genius, you realize you can marry the datasets into one result for every illness. Since the product is using structured data, much of it could be built at scale without the need to create pages manually.

This new resource would be useful for anyone making decisions about which insurance to buy and what their out-of-pocket costs might be for various chronic or surprise illnesses. Yes, there is competition for this product from less complete datasets, but market share will grow as more people become aware of it. An initial PR push might help to get the ball rolling on links that will help search visibility, but eventually, there will be branded search, too, as users look for this most complete dataset. Non-branded queries will consist of all illnesses combined with a cost or price keyword. As the product grows, there could be iterations that incorporate more things beyond price, but at least from the outset, you have validated that there's lots of demand.

Zooming in on this product, there are many aspects that make it an ideal Product-Led SEO strategy. It is programmatic and scalable, creates something new, and addresses untapped search demand. Additionally, and most importantly, there is a direct path to a paying telehealth user. Users can access the data without being a current customer, but the cost differential between telehealth (when appropriate) versus in-person will lead some users down a discovery journey that ends with a conversion. A user who might never have considered telehealth might be drawn to the cost savings in reduced transportation and waiting times that they would never have known about had they not seen your content.

Making a Decision

Now, as the telehealth executive, you have two competing product ideas to choose from. While you can eventually do both, you can only do one at a time, as I suggested earlier. You will take both of these product ideas and spec out all the requirements. The conditions library might require buying a medical repository and licensing many stock photos, while the cost directory is built on open-source datasets. Additionally, they will each have different technical requirements, which might mean divergent hiring needs to build them.

Once you make the decision, there really is no looking back, as there will never be a point of comparison about how the rejected option might have done. You can't compare against a hypothetical. During this process, it will be quite obvious that the build process will be lengthy and expensive, but you should take solace in the fact that it will be even more expensive for anyone to copy you. You are building a figurative moat around your product-and-acquisition strategy. The success of this effort will cement your brand in the eyes of millions. While most of those who will use your product will never pay you, you have tapped into a juggernaut of paying customers who didn't even know they needed your primary telehealth offering.

Now, with your deeper understanding of Product-Led SEO, we can take a look at examples of companies that have done a fantastic job of using this strategy as their recipe for exponential growth. Anyone can create content for search, but these companies created products for search users.

PRODUCT-LED SEO SUCCESSES

Rather than relying on keywords and content as the bedrock of their SEO efforts, some mammoth internet corporations have used a scaled approach, relying more on Product-Led SEO and engineering than marketing. Amazon, TripAdvisor, Zillow, and even Wikipedia are strong examples of Product-Led SEO, but there are thousands of others.

Before each of these four companies developed and propagated their products on the internet, there wasn't even keyword research for them to rely on.

AMAZON

Amazon focused on building a great architecture to support a well-indexed site even before the idea of SEO existed. The Amazon site has grown into the SEO magnet it is today by scaling that initial iteration of a well-developed product that fit with SEO principles.

Had it relied on keyword research to launch the site in the early days of the internet, it may have over-prioritized the adult keywords that were so popular on the internet at that time. This choice of keywords would have been to the detriment of the well of book searchers that were just waiting for the right pages to be relevant to their queries.

TRIPADVISOR

TripAdvisor didn't start by creating a "blog" of reviews of the most popular hotels with the most search volumes.

Instead, this site built an architecture that could scale and host reviews for every property in the entire world. It took years before TripAdvisor outranked individual travel blogs and pre-existing sites. The blogs already ranked highly on search for the most popular properties. TripAdvisor took a different tactic. Its reward is that today it ranks in the top five of results for every hotel in the world.

ZILLOW

Zillow didn't focus all its SEO efforts on trying to rank for the popular keywords in its space, perhaps words like "home value" or "online realtor." Instead, Zillow poured its efforts into building a colossal site that has a page for every single address in the

United States. At the time, such overkill may have seemed like a foolish approach. First, no one looked for specific addresses. Second, at the time, it would have been competing with Google Maps or even MapQuest, which was still a thing.

Now, Zillow has a mammoth footprint visible in organic search for every address in the country. It could not have made a more profitable bet.

WIKIPEDIA

Wikipedia didn't set out to merely be an online dictionary or encyclopedia that only had articles for the terms most people were searching for online at the time. Rather, Wikipedia set out to be an encyclopedia of *everything*. It set out to be the go-to for searching the who, what, where, when, how, and why of anything.

Early in Wikipedia's process, having an entry for everything might have seemed like an absolute impossibility. It disregarded the naysayers and built a product that could continuously scale into a repository of everything in every language. Of course, there are gaps in its knowledge base, and there probably always will be, but it has been undeniably successful at achieving its goal.

BUILDING ON SUCCESS

Like product-led growth, where user experiences drive adoption of products, feedback from search engines drives future iterations of SEO. To put this into context, there are many popular companies, like Shopify, Dropbox, and Slack, that built products so fantastic and useful their users became their evangelists and brought others onto the platform. Rather than invest resources into sales, these organizations focused on continuously improving the product experience so current users would bring in even more potential customers.

This very same mechanism can and should work for SEO. Build an experience that is useful for users first, and the search engines will follow. As we discussed previously, search engines use AI to mimic humans, and a great human experience is rewarded by search algorithms.

When we know what resonates on search with both search engines and users, we can allow that knowledge to influence our future roadmap of improvements and adjacent products. We can build on existing success.

Amazon does not need to make the same SEO leap of faith as it enters new categories these days because Amazon has built the architecture to be confident it will get organic traffic on anything it launches.

TripAdvisor's success in hotel reviews gave it a playbook on how to launch Things to Do. Zillow's dominance in address search opened up the pathway to organic visibility in mortgage searches, which had always been one of the most competitive categories on the web. Success leads to success.

THE TWENTY-YEAR WINNER

With the clarity of only creating what users seek, Product-Led SEO will always be the clear winner. Rather than building SEO assets aimed at search algorithms or keywords, SEO is built around what the user wants. However, when first starting an SEO effort, it is undoubtedly challenging to envision the success you might see from this approach. It looks like a tremendous and uncertain investment.

It is my opinion that there can be a Product-Led SEO angle in every vertical and niche. However, pulling off that work successfully will likely require monumental work by Engineering teams to build a product that will eventually become an SEO juggernaut. You will need a great degree of patience and even faith. You won't be able to see the end from the beginning.

At the outset, it will not be clear that there will be demand for the eventual product, but remember, there was no data supporting the eventual SEO goals of Amazon, TripAdvisor, Zillow, or Wikipedia either. The best point for Product-Led SEO is that after companies are successful with their product-first efforts, they have built a defensive moat that makes it very difficult for competitors to unseat them. Think how difficult it might be for a new website to create real-estate valuations like Zillow, e-commerce like Amazon, or hotel reviews like TripAdvisor.

In our hypothetical telehealth example from earlier in the chapter, regardless of which product you decided to build, you would be creating that product category. (We are assuming no other comprehensive directory of every embarrassing condition or all-inclusive-pricing library exists.) By you creating either of these products, you will be tapping into demand that no one else knew existed. By the time any competitors notice you have invented a new acquisition source, you will be many months to years ahead of them.

You will also have the knowledge of how and why your product resonates with the customer base that they will never have.

Amazon, Zillow, TripAdvisor, and Wikipedia have lots of copy-cats, but they still stay steps ahead. If you tap into unmatched demand for a product, your telehealth company will sit in this same luxurious position.

While much of the effort around building a Product-Led SEO effort naturally revolves around the product and building aspects, that's not to say there is no place for content. Rather, the content included as a part of this and any SEO effort must be the right kind of content.

CONTENT FOR SEO

Bill Gates is credited with coining the phrase "Content is King" in 1996. He wrote the phrase in an essay, where he explained why Microsoft was partnering with NBC, predicting that content providers would be in the best position to monetize the nascent internet. He wanted to put Microsoft in a position to benefit from what he perceived to be the greatest future profit potential.

On this topic, Gates' prediction was only partially right. Yes, content producers can harness the vastness of the internet for financial gain. However, some of the web's biggest companies earn vast sums from others' content, which they just aggregate: Google, Facebook, Spotify, Netflix, and so on.

LOW-QUALITY CONTENT

Bill Gates' thesis was about the type of high-quality, exclusive content produced by a media conglomerate like NBC. Unfortunately, the phrase "Content is King" has become a part of the marketing lexicon without distinction. All sorts of marketing books, conference presentations, and trainings exhort marketers to focus on content as the most important component of any marketing effort.

Somehow, this idea became a call to arms to just create content without any bar of quality. Marketers have fallen in line, flooding the internet with the kind of garbage that makes you dumber for reading or viewing it. You wish you could turn back the clock to reclaim the minutes you wasted.

The world is awash in rambling audio, shaky video, and the worst travesty of all: poorly written long-form content written for SEO.

DOES IT EVEN WORK?

The belief is that somehow this content will draw people in from various channels. Then, once they are on the site, somehow, they will be trapped into buying, calling, filling out a lead, or whatever the KPI might be.

The problem is endemic across all verticals. Take a moment and do a search on Google for luxury hotels, and then read the descriptions of the rooms. You will find many examples of content that reads as if it was written by someone with a keyword goal. I once read a room description for a luxury hotel that mentioned there was a bathtub with water that came out of a faucet. Try the same for jewelry stores. It gets even worse when you look at websites for local small businesses.

Bad content isn't confined to a specific marketing medium, but it is less prevalent on paid channels. Paid and brand marketers are smart enough to know if you spend money on your marketing, it will defeat the purpose to have customers repulsed by useless content.

CONTENT WORKED TO THE BONE

Every day, content producers (whether in-house or outsourced) are given the kinds of goals that might be given to a warehouse worker packing boxes. X amount of content needs to be produced per day that must contain Y words and use Z keywords. This prescription-type of content is not a king; it is an indentured servant expected to work magic that it is simply not equipped to do.

Imagine if some of the greatest media stories of the last century had been written in this framework. If the TV shows of the previous decades had been walk-and-talk videos, would TV watching have become a family affair? If newspapers of the past had been filled with infographics that forced you to turn page after page after page of force-fed advertisements, would anyone even read today? I think not.

CONTENT IS SELLING

I assume creating content for content's sake works for some websites and products, but it seems a terrible way of selling anything. Using low-quality content as a teaser is like walking into a high-end store and first being shown the cheap knockoffs as an enticement to keep going deeper into the establishment where someone *might* reveal something real. It wouldn't work offline. Why do it online?

Personally, I think content should be considered with the same gravitas as deploying a highly paid salesperson. Just as no business would allow itself to be represented by a slurring, sloppy drunk, no business should let poor-quality content be its first impression to potential customers. Businesses are always diligent in tracking the performance of every salesperson and paying out appropriate commissions. Content should be treated similarly. Content should never be deployed and then not measured. Unlike other marketing methods, content is inherently trackable. It should earn its keep.

USER-CENTERED CONTENT

A good salesperson targets their approach with a specific person in mind. Content also needs to be written with the end user in mind. If there is no added value for a user, the content should be deemed useless. Smart readers will see through the veil of sentences strung together for no purpose other than to garner a click.

I think we need to put an end to the idea that content is king and, therefore, writing content is an end unto itself. Content is a business tool like any other. When content is correctly viewed as an instrument of success, setting arbitrary goals on content seems even more ridiculous. Only a fool would mandate spending a set amount on paid advertising even if it never converted, yet these kinds of objectives are commonplace around content.

CONTENT IS A TOOL

Not every tool is right for every scenario, and content is not always required. Restaurants don't need long-form content describing their ingredients just so they might get SEO traffic. Not every doctor's office website needs to replicate the medical library of WebMD. Small, service-based businesses do not need a blog. Not every business needs an active social media following. This might be digital marketing heresy, but not all businesses even need a website. A local business will get more customers on Google My Business than they might on a poorly built website with weak content.

The resources wasted on bad content are better spent in channels that will actually reach customers and bring in revenue. Deployed effectively, content can have an ROI in the thousands of percent over many years, but content with no purpose will never have any return. Content is a tremendously powerful tool in the hands of the right marketer. It should be wielded effectively and revered, not made to toil as an indentured servant.

If content is the product of a website, and the goal of the website is for readers to consume that content, creating words for the sake of a word count or keyword goal is an utter waste of time. Product-Led SEO requires thinking of the reader and why they should spend their precious time enjoying the content.

The same idea will apply to how the content is structured from a website-architecture standpoint. If internal links are driven by just satisfying search engine requirements rather than helping the user/reader discover other interesting articles to read, the links are useless from a business standpoint. Every detail should focus on the user/reader.

You can't focus on search engine bots and expect the user to also be satisfied, but you absolutely CAN rely on the search engines following along if you focus on the user. In SEO, there will always be two distinct audiences: the search engine and the user. Search engines need words—even ones that don't make sense to the user—but they can only reward you with high positions on Google. It is the users who need sensible products (in any fashion), and they are the ones who initiate the transactions that lead to business success. Product-Led SEO requires you to think of the user first and the search engine second. A user focus requires a human touch and is not something that can be machine or software driven.

CHAPTER THREE

SEO IS A JOB
FOR HUMANS

When I joined SurveyMonkey in 2012, there was very little unbranded search (queries that did not use the brand name in it); however, there were four solid generic keywords sending traffic: "survey," "surveys," "online survey," and "online surveys." As a result of its history and authority on the internet, Survey-Monkey was in the first position for all four of those keywords, and they were responsible for sending a lot of traffic to the website.

In late 2013, I noticed that in the UK, the positions for two of these keywords, "surveys" and "online surveys," had slipped from position one to position nine. The new ranking results were websites that offered to pay people reward points for taking surveys. When compared to SurveyMonkey's authority and brand, these sites of dubious quality should never have been able to achieve those positions. To understand the situation better, I thoroughly researched the backlinks, technical architecture, and content of all the top-ten results for these queries.

After turning over every possible stone, I came up with the only logical conclusion: when it came to the plural versions of those queries, Google had determined a user's intent in searching them was to find a place to take a survey rather than to create a survey. While this problem had been isolated to the UK only, I felt the problem would eventually migrate to the US, too, and cause an impact on traffic everywhere. After first showing up in results in Australia and then Canada, within six months, this ranking change had, in fact, reached the search results in the United States. I had been right, unfortunately.

(Note: SurveyMonkey's position on these keywords has since improved, but the majority of the results on these keywords are still survey-taking websites. This means Google has adjusted the way it views the intent here, reflecting the possibility a user searching either of these terms could want to take OR create a survey.)

Had I just relied on the SEO software I was using at the time, I might still be convinced there was something wrong in the technical execution of SurveyMonkey's targeting for these terms. Based on quantitative metrics, every SEO tool would have assumed that no survey-taking websites could overtake SurveyMonkey.com. The tools would focus on the technical details and miss out on the intent data behind the query that only Google knows and a perceptive search marketer would notice. SEO tools are great, but human intelligence is better.

There are several SEO tools I use daily; without them, I would not be able to work effectively on any SEO projects. Yet, I think tools are just that—devices to help complete a project. Gadgets, gizmos, and gimmicks are not a solution in and of themselves. They cannot be. There may one day be areas where

AI will supplant humans and be able to do a job beginning to end without human intervention. But anything in the realm of Product and marketing must have human input.

SEO IS LIKE CONSTRUCTION

I'll explain my opinion with an analogy to home construction. Most construction workers would likely believe their jobs cannot be completely automated. However, it's not farfetched to imagine robots could take over once each task is broken down. There are devices that can hammer nails automatically, hold walls straight, and even follow a schematic to build a frame.

For now, there is no single robot hammer that can crawl across a house frame and know exactly where to hammer in a nail—but years ago, there wasn't a robot that could vacuum a house either. It is entirely possible that one day an inventor will create robots that can be guided by a repetitive algorithm to do monotonous, labor-intensive tasks more cheaply and safely than humans can.

However, there is one area of construction that will never be replaced by a robot, and that is the architecture. A robot will never be able to understand the human emotions and personal choices that go into deciding how a home should be designed.

The robot can decide where the front door should be and how big the walk-in closet can be—but a human will disagree with the aesthetics or function and change the arbitrary robot decisions. A robot can certainly build a perfect set of blueprints to spec—but it can't translate desire into a plan.

The same concept applies to SEO and marketing. Yes, one day, there may be tools that construct the perfect website based on findings about what works in search. The future software may generate the best keyword ideas and maybe even write the content. But we will always need the human element. Without it, something would always be missing.

At best, software can mimic what others seem to be doing well, but humans can have creative ideas on how to get ahead. Even further, while software can write content based on keywords—which may even appear well in search—that content will lack the emotion necessary to resonate with humans. People need to be able to engage with that content. They need to resonate with it; they need to feel.

AUTOMATIC SEO

Every once in a while, there's an article about a tool that does SEO "automatically" getting a round of funding. There's usually some breathless proclamation about how the contraption or device will disrupt the entire industry. Ironically, all these articles neglect to mention the AI that already exists.

Google is already using AI to understand and rank content. The way to "beat" Google's AI will never be to duel with another AI tool. The way to succeed will be to put a human in the mix.

Until we live in a world where robots do all our shopping, SEO could never be entirely disrupted by software. If all SEO could be distilled down into doing keyword research and structuring web pages, perhaps SEO might one day be able to be done entirely by software. However, successful SEO is so much more than those basics. Good, strategic SEO includes knowing how to architect a website into folders and files, the types of content to create, and the personas of the potential users (we will touch on this later); learning from performance to optimize for growth; and, most of all, building a product that resonates with real users.

Think about all the most successful sites on the web, and then imagine if it were possible to replicate their success. Could a machine have built Wikipedia? Would automated reviews have helped Yelp, TripAdvisor, or Amazon win their categories? Would Google News be a dominant source of news if all it did was index machine-written content?

Humans would never have adopted these sites in such numbers if machines had built the strategy, websites, and content. Anyone looking to replicate the success of these giants would be better served by finding the smartest humans they can to create something compelling rather than looking for the next automated shiny object.

All the sites that try to only use software to manage their SEO leave a gaping hole for human-driven campaigns to beat them in search visibility. They are copying what everyone else does rather than strategically figuring out the next thing that works.

Software can't figure out how to do the next big thing. Similarly, relying on software to diagnose your SEO problems, or even tell you that you have SEO problems, is asking for trouble. Getting an accurate view of where you are always requires a human.

SEO AUDITS

I was once talking to an entrepreneur about accelerating the SEO performance on his site, and I suggested he might want to get an SEO site audit to understand what is presently working and where there might be issues. He immediately rejected that idea, saying, "We already have Moz, so we are good." The fact that he didn't get the distinction between a tool and an audit made me realize a lot of people probably are equally unaware.

Software tools aren't people. While Moz and other tools, like Ahrefs, SEMrush, Conductor, Clarity, and Searchmetrics, are all great for seeing progress, they don't have the human intellect necessary to clarify the why or why not behind the metrics. A better way of understanding this is to use a health analogy.

Basic wearable devices like Fitbits are great to help you keep on top of common health stats like activity, heart rate, and sleep. However, the numbers are no substitute for a full physical checkup by a medical professional. Your heartrate device will not find an artery blockage. In a similar way, a daily SEO stat tracker, like the tools above, report well on activity metrics, but they will not catch an impending sitewide SEO "heart attack." Creeping URL changes or misconfigured canonical links could blow up suddenly, and neither will be caught by software.

No one should rely on WebMD for a diagnosis. Similarly, when a website is experiencing an organic issue, the last thing anyone should do is rely on a status report from a tool. This is the time to have an experienced professional have a look at the site and conduct an audit to find out what's ailing it.

WHAT DOES A WEBSITE AUDIT LOOK FOR?

There are basic templates for a website audit that any experienced SEO professional will use to start; however, once they've dug into the metrics, the person will follow the indicators into an individualized audit. When you visit a doctor, you want someone with lots of experience and an innate sense of the best questions to ask; with SEO audits, it is the same.

The concept of an SEO audit has been somewhat abused in an SEO industry that has shady websites offering quickie audits for $100. An audit was never meant to be just a checklist to put on a wall poster. An audit should be a careful look at your entire SEO effort from an experienced practitioner. It is a very human task.

The more experienced the person or team conducting the audit is, the more they will be able to zero in on what's wrong and understand how (and where) to look deeper. An experienced person or team will also know which audit to pursue. A general SEO audit will look at many of the different areas listed below, while a competitive audit will examine competitors' SEO strategies. A technical audit digs into technical architecture, whereas a backlink audit only looks at a website's backlink portfolio.

An audit, especially for a site that has never engaged in any SEO efforts, is meant to be a deep look into areas where SEO can be improved. For sites that are experiencing an SEO change, good or bad, an audit is an opportunity to dig into the drivers of that change. An audit can be conducted by anyone with enough experience to know what they are looking for, and there is not always a reason to engage an external party if there is an employee with the requisite knowledge to conduct an audit.

OPTIMAL AUDIT AREAS

As we've said, each audit will ultimately diverge as the auditor follows the site's architecture. However, every audit will include at least a look at these high-level areas.

Penalty analysis—Are there any unexplained drop-offs in metrics that align with either Google manual actions or known algorithmic updates?

URL structure—Do URLs have a nice, clean structure to make it clear to both users and search engines what is contained on each page? (Ideally, there shouldn't be any parameters in the URL, but this can depend on the specific use cases.)

Duplicate content and canonical usage—Duplicate-content issues cause Google to have to make a decision about which URL to index. This may not be the desired URL, so canonicals can help declare the preferred URL. Improper usage of canonicals can be very detrimental to the site. There are those that call this a duplicate-content penalty, but it is actually not a penalty at all, as this is how search indexation is designed to work.

Internal links—Are internal links in good working order for proper crawling and indexation? (In many respects, internal links can be more important than external links, so this step is critical.)

Backlinks—Which sites link to our site, and are they helping or hurting us? For a big site, understanding the mix of backlinks can be an audit unto itself.

Indexation—Is the site properly indexed in search? What is holding it back? In my opinion, this is the most important part of any audit.

Script usage—Which scripts are being used, and what are the implications? Despite Google's proclamations to the contrary, using JavaScript is simply not as effective for SEO as HTML.

Uncovering JavaScript that drives important parts of the site can lead to new opportunities for growth if recoded in a more crawler-friendly fashion.

Keyword usage—What keywords are being used, and what gaps exist? Keywords are the bulwark of any SEO campaign, and mapping them can often lead to opportunities.

On-Page SEO—What title tags (titles, descriptions, H1, H2, etc.) are being used? Good title tags are the basis of any effort, and it is always surprising to me how many opportunities can be uncovered by spending time on their usage.

Content quality—What content is being used, and of what quality? SEO is driven by content, but poor content can actually be harmful. An outsider's view can assess the quality accurately.

Robots.txt—How effective are the directions to search engines on what pages of the site can be crawled? Overdoing it will lead to important pages without traffic, while underdoing it will lead to useless pages being crawled.

Sitemaps—How effective are the current XML and HTML sitemaps? They are both helpful and necessary for page discovery, and this analysis will point out opportunities to improve the current setup.

Site speed—How fast do pages and the site load? Page and site speeds are factored into the Google algorithm for very slow sites, but even if there's no algorithmic issue, very slow loads will lead to a poor user experience and, therefore, poor conversions.

Expired content—Are any content or products being shown

to search engines and users who are no longer relevant? How these pages are handled can have a significant impact on a site.

Spam—Is there any? Even the most authoritative and secure websites have had issues with spam. While this likely will not lead to a search-performance issue, it is certainly not a good user experience.

Schema markup—Where are the current markup and the available markup to help us find new opportunities for growth? In a world of voice assistants, schema markup is increasingly more important, as it helps search engines understand context.

Mobile versus desktop—How will mobile search experiences interact with the site? Mobile devices often approach search in fundamentally different ways, so there should be no surprise that mobile SEO can be different, too. This analysis reveals those differences.

International—How do all the areas above function in different countries? An international audit can be a standalone audit since, depending on how many countries are targeted, this can be a very broad exercise. Also, if there are many language variants, you might need multiple international audits to ensure all languages are covered.

AUDIT BEST PRACTICES

Whether you decide to hire an expert or conduct your own audit, always make sure you identify issues that have an impact on visibility. Do not just rely on the quick health checkup of a tool.

When deciding what to fix, prioritize based on impact. An

SEO audit is a health checkup to generate a baseline of how a site measures up against SEO best practices; yet, having a site with a perfect SEO score does not mean the site is primed to unleash torrents of traffic. There are many websites that would fail an SEO best-practices test but still do very well on search. Similarly, there are websites that check every SEO box but hardly generate any SEO traffic.

The most important takeaway from any SEO audit is the "so what." There's no point in just declaring a site has a set architecture, for example, unless there's an action that should be followed up on it.

I have seen audits run on for over one hundred pages but are light on action items. Creating a useless book doesn't do the creator or the recipient any good. To this end, the audit (if one is going to be created) should be done by someone who can really uncover the action items. The best scenario is an internal employee, as the audit will guide them in their understanding of the website as they do their job.

A second-best option is to hire a consultant who will be partnered with an internal team (in any function) to dig into a website's search visibility and convey action items to the right teams. The goal should be to uncover action items in the clearest way possible rather than provide a thick book or checklist. The decision regarding who to hire is likely one that needs to be made by the executive who oversees SEO.

In the following pages, I will offer some advice to anyone looking to hire a consultant or employee to aid with SEO audits or SEO efforts in general. Because SEO is a task done by humans, who you work with is of utmost importance, and how and when you should hire are critical decisions.

Here are my recommendations.

FOR EXECUTIVES: HIRING A CONSULTANT VERSUS A FULL-TIME EMPLOYEE

(While most of this book is intended for those with hands-on access to SEO efforts, I have included a few sections, like this one, intended for executives who currently or will support SEO and need to make decisions about how best to do so.)

As an organization decides it wants to start focusing on SEO, the first decision it makes is around who should do that work. For many larger companies, the first inclination is to hire someone internally who will devote most of their time to SEO efforts. For most companies, this is a mistake.

Early in a company's organic-traffic journey, there aren't forty hours a week of work that can be done on SEO. Most early-stage SEO efforts need to be on strategy, involving internal and external research as well as thinking. Even after the company pivots into actioning on the plans, SEO may not be a full-time job.

Given these realities, there are a few options on how to move forward on an SEO effort, and I will dissect the pros and cons of each.

1. **Hire a full-time person internally**—Choosing to hire someone has its own decision tree. A first hire can be experienced, with the goal of eventually growing a team and taking a leadership role. Or it could be a junior hire that will need to scale into the role. There are challenges with each option. The senior person will be significantly more

expensive, harder to hire, and challenging to retain; however, they will implement a strategy and process that is tried and proven. A junior person will be less costly and quicker to hire, but depending on their experience in SEO, they may make errors that will be costly to fix later on.

2. **Hire a full-time contractor**—The decisions around making this hire are similar to hiring someone in a full-time salaried role. (A contractor has budget advantages.) The one notable item here is that SEO talent is in very high demand, so any experienced hire willing to acquiesce to a contract instead of a stable role may have specific reasons worth exploring before making the hire. On the junior-person side, using a contractor allows a company to be more nimble, but the employee will be far less incentivized to grow their SEO abilities over time.

3. **Hire a project-based consultant**—A project-based consultant is an expert brought on just to solve a particular problem. Once that issue is solved, the engagement terminates. Using a consultant instead of a full-time employee gives the company the flexibility to get exactly what it needs for the desired timeframe. There are many great options, and companies should find someone who has specific experience in their industry and can offer the outcomes they are seeking. When choosing to hire a consultant, finding the right fit should trump budget concerns. One additional spin on consultants is that a company can hire someone on a fixed, monthly retainer. This person can often provide the decision-making expertise for significantly less than a full-time employee. Consulting rates should always be evaluated by whether a person can provide the same output as a full-time employee for similar or less cost.

4. **Hire an agency**—There are hundreds of agencies, big and small, that offer SEO services. Agencies will typically come

in at a lower all-in cost than an individual consultant or employee, but they will also potentially provide less value. An agency should be chosen on the basis of the specific outcomes promised in a proposal and the caliber of the people who will be working on the account. It is a common agency practice to showcase star employees during the sales process but then task junior employees to manage the account. Ensure this will not happen by making a request for specific employees to work on the account.

Early-stage companies often hire a general marketer who does paid, social, and organic efforts as part of the same job, but this means they aren't going to have particularly strong skills in any one arena. I personally advise against this, as it's a lot of money to spend on mediocre decision-making. If you are in this spot, I recommend contracting a paid-search and/or social expert(s) first and later an SEO expert separately. Definitely don't focus on doing it yourself if you are the leader who faces a significant learning curve; you'll get further by focusing on the coordination and your existing skills rather than the specialty work you can outsource.

(Don't mistake reading blog posts or SEO guides as having the education you will need to make the right SEO decisions. Yes, you should absolutely read and learn as much as possible about SEO, but if SEO is going to be a critical channel for you, don't rely on just your own knowledge. You wouldn't code your key product after watching a few YouTube videos. Paid, social, and SEO are of equal importance and should be treated as such.)

As you decide which internal or external resource you want to work with, ensure the person or agency will help you level up your own knowledge in a way that drives growth. Don't just get an audit and file it away. Find someone who will have the same goals you will have on growth. If you don't have goals, work with the teams to create those goals.

Most importantly, any external resource will need a dedicated person or people on your team to help get things done. This point of contact could be a marketer, engineer, C-suite executive, or just a junior SEO specialist. If you don't currently have a good point of contact who will help drive SEO work internally, you should make a fresh hire. I would suggest this person have great project-management skills, as they will be helping your external resource, and eventually your internal resource, simply get stuff done.

Depending on how the company grows, this project manager could also be the liaison for other consultants who fill gaps where full-time employees might not make the most sense. For example, unless you are managing a very large paid-marketing budget, I would counsel against having a full-time Paid-Marketing team or person. An agency would be far more cost-effective and successful, but they will also need a dedicated point of contact. If your new hire is a skilled project manager, they can help coordinate paid and organic marketing without ever having a background in either discipline, and a project-management skillset is more advantageous to cross-disciplinary coordination later as the SEO leader grows into the role down the line.

Keep in mind, it might not make sense for a company to focus on SEO at all in its early stages, especially if the company is still growing. Many times, it is too early to invest any effort into SEO that might be put to better use in another function. For example, before a company reaches the point of diminishing returns on their paid-marketing spend, they should be returning at least $2 for every $1 they spend. If funding is pulled from paid marketing to invest in a longer-term SEO initiative, growth of the company could be handicapped.

I always recommend early-stage companies first spend as much as they are comfortable allocating toward paid marketing before they shift to SEO. Paid marketing will help quickly determine product-market fit, identify customer journeys, and, most importantly, generate revenue. Knowledge gained from paid marketing will help SEO maximize its success. Whereas, if SEO is built out before this knowledge is gained, you might be using only assumptions rather than hard data.

It is true SEO will eventually be the most profitable marketing channel, but the company first has to reach a stage where it can have other profitable channels to drive immediate growth. During early stages, SEO will likely not be the best investment option.

If your company is ready to invest in SEO, it makes sense for your stage, and you've decided on a full-time employee, here are some things to think about in the hiring process.

FOR EXECUTIVES: HOW TO HIRE A FULL-TIME SEO EMPLOYEE

As the demand for organic growth skyrockets, there will be an increasing number of SEO job requests being created. Many of the job descriptions sound like the hiring manager has an SEO problem that needs to be solved, and they don't really know what they are looking for. Some of the postings have responsibilities that may have been copied from job requests that are ten years old.

For example, there are job descriptions that look for people with experience on social-bookmarking sites. Social bookmarking used to be a popular method that probably didn't actually work as a way to build backlinks to a site. In today's SEO paradigm, this would be a complete waste of time even if there were still social-bookmarking sites. There are other job descriptions that look like they are looking for a copywriter who can write words that are "SEOed." (Copywriting is a whole different topic.)

Finally, with the number of actual job requirements that are included in the description, many postings are looking for someone who understands 1) content, 2) project management, 3) engineering, and 4) analytics. Finding a person with all these divergent skills might be an impossible mission.

DECIDE WHO YOU NEED

To crack hiring the right person to fill an SEO need, you need to take a step back and truly understand the need that you have. Within SEO, there will be people who are amazing at strategy and somewhat weak on tactics and others with the opposite skills. Depending on the needs of a company, there may be lots of people to act on SEO recommendations, but an overall strategy is missing. In that case, you may want to hire a strategist.

The type of SEO person you need will depend on the gaps you have. You don't want to end up having a strong tactical person but no one to develop the overall strategy. Most strategists will have some tactical abilities, but not all tactical people will have strategy skills. Think carefully.

Strategy and tactics are not the only distinctions. The skill strengths of SEO practitioners can be broken into four distinct functional areas. Whom you should hire is entirely dependent on your individual company's existing SEO abilities and gaps.

1. **Product management**—This is someone who can conceptualize ways to develop a substantial product-value add for organic users and coordinate the team to build it. This individual will have strong prioritization and communication abilities. They must also have innate customer empathy to know exactly what a user might want.
2. **Copywriter**—A person with strong writing abilities who is able to create content using keywords and attract organic users with ease.
3. **Technical**—This is someone who likely has coding abilities (trained or self-taught) and can develop solutions that require complex technical decisions. They will not be a full engineer but will know enough about coding to convey requests to engineers and be able to recognize faulty code to highlight to engineers.
4. **PR**—A PR-oriented person is most useful when the challenge faced by a company centers on increasing links to existing content. This person will have strong people skills and communication abilities.

Finding someone who has experience and skills in all these areas is not impossible, but it is not easy. It's far more effective to take a step back and determine exactly what the company will need and where there is bandwidth to get things done.

Earlier-stage companies should ideally hire a jack-of-all-trades with varying skills across Marketing and Product. Younger companies likely don't have enough SEO needs to keep a full-time employee busy, so having a number of functional areas for this hire to work on will work out best. Later-stage companies with many employees are better served by a person with deep experience in just SEO.

In later-stage companies where the new hire will only work on SEO projects, prioritizing skill sets is critical. It is highly unlikely to find someone who is perfect in every area. You can balance between where existing employees can compensate for skill gaps in a new hire or areas where you might want to make another new hire. There is no perfect formula for how to hire and which skills to prioritize, as the specifics will always be individual to each company.

COMPENSATION

What should be plainly obvious from this diversity of skills and requirements is that compensation for your first SEO marketer will cover a very wide range. I don't believe it is helpful to declare the ideal salary in this book, nor do I think anyone should make such declarations. From experience, I have never seen the many public surveys on SEO salaries be in line with real in-house compensation packages; therefore, I would take them with a grain of salt.

Large enterprises will have salary ladders that place SEO managers within a job category with some of the more common placements under Product management, Product marketing, content producers, performance marketers, or online marketers. Obviously, total compensation will be based on experience but will also range based on the job category. Product management will have the highest salaries, while content producers will have the lowest.

Smaller companies that do not use formal compensation ladders should align SEO salaries with one of the other more common job functions when setting up compensation packages. You may have more flexibility in how much or little you pay, but use those other job functions as a benchmark. One thing that should be avoided, at all costs, is making any part of the salary variable based on a KPI. This will lead toward the wrong incentives and not help prioritize your SEO efforts in the right direction of long-term, sustainable growth. I have seen SEO bonuses aligned with link metrics, ranking positions, clicks from search, and even revenue, and in every case, it caused long-term issues. The saying "what gets measured gets done" is exactly what happens in these scenarios, often with far-reaching, negative impacts.

As SEO is going to be a critical part of your growth, don't look to pay as little as possible because you will get what you pay for. While this section discusses hiring a full-time employee to drive SEO growth, I believe you should have the same approach toward compensation when you hire a contractor, consultant, or agency. Consider the costs of the external party based on what you would have to pay someone internally, and that should be your deciding factor.

SEO is a build-and-grow challenge, so pay for time and mind-share rather than deliverables, KPIs, and even hours. Typically, this equates to a monthly retainer, but there can be adjustments based on a minimum of hours worked or milestones achieved. Again, I would recommend you use these intermediate metrics the same way you might for a full-time employee on salary. You wouldn't fire an employee who did not achieve measurable results in just one month provided they at least put in the requisite time. An external team should be judged on the same scale.

With all of the above in mind, the hiring manager can write the ideal job description and interview candidates who can solve that particular need, and the new hire will have an impact where it really makes a difference.

BEST PRACTICES ON WRITING THE JOB DESCRIPTION

1. Determine what the end goal should be. A new site launched? Growth in content? Organic visibility?
2. Try to break down the steps that might be necessary to get to that end goal. These are the specific requirements that should be in the job description.
3. Understand what sort of reporting might be necessary to know when that goal is reached. Require familiarity with that tool.
4. Decide what sort of hard skills the person needs. If you want a link builder, they don't need a math background. If you want a technical SEO specialist, they don't need to be a great communicator.
5. Know whether you want a senior or junior hire, and include appropriate years of experience.
6. Understand what kind of previous jobs provide the ideal background for your hire. Do they need experience in a big company? Agency? Early-stage company?
7. Include some "nice to have" other skills, but really believe they are not requirements.

With proper preparation before opening up the job listing, you will make sifting through resumes and deciding who to hire much easier. Because you have clearly defined what the new hire will be doing once they are on board, it will also be a lot easier to make the decision on who is the best candidate.

INTERVIEWING SEO CANDIDATES

Once you have decided what type of SEO person you want on your team, you will have a better sense of the skillset they will need. Based on that skillset, you can begin crafting an interview process and questions to ask during the interviews.

Process

To find the best fit, every SEO candidate should always meet with all their potential counterparts, even if they are not on the same team. Interviewers from these respective teams should assess both hard skills—can they do the job?—and soft skills—will the team be able to work with them? The number of actual interviewers will depend on the norms for a company, but if a large number of interviews is standard, I suggest the following interviewers. If a company is smaller or limited on time, ensure you have interviewers who can assess all four areas of Product, content, technical, and PR mentioned in the previous paragraphs.

- **Product managers**—Hires who will focus on building a product and the technical aspects of SEO should meet someone on the Product team. The product manager they would be working with should interview the SEO candidate as if they are being added to their team. They should ask questions on a variety of soft and hard skills.
- **Business Intelligence or Data Science**—This is the team that will be responsible for reporting on SEO metrics and building measurement tools. This team should assess the SEO candidates' analytical abilities as well as whether they will be easy to work with. If there isn't a dedicated Data Science team or counterpart, analytical questions should be included by other interviewers.

- **Marketing counterparts**—It's always helpful to have potential team members confirm they are able to work with a new hire. If the company is large, and it is not feasible to have many marketers meeting with candidates, at a minimum, the person responsible for paid marketing should meet with all potential SEO hires. SEO and paid marketing are very similar from a performance standpoint, and the paid marketer would be best positioned to assess a search skillset.
- **Content**—Depending on the company, an SEO team might own, be on, or just work adjacent to the Content team. Regardless of whether the SEO candidate is a technical, product, content, or link hire, writing is a critical skill that should be a requirement for any hire. The interviewers should assess the candidate's writing abilities and soft skills on how they communicate with writers.
- **Senior executives**—This is not applicable for all hires, but senior hires should be assessed on whether they have executive presence. Will they be able to communicate with executives directly, or do they need to go through their manager? Most importantly, SEO should be considered a mission-critical process within a company, and having executives sign off on SEO hires keeps the sense of mission on the radar.
- **Frontend engineering**—Frontend engineers will be building and fulfilling the requests from the SEO Engineering team. In interviews, they should determine the candidates' abilities to communicate their requests to engineers and make complete asks that don't require engineers to continuously request more details.
- **Backend engineering**—Backend engineers are responsible for building server-side code as well as handling any redirects. Only the technically-minded SEO candidates need to be assessed by backend engineers, and the questioning

should probe how much they understand about various technologies and tools.

- QA—Any technical or Product-centric SEO needs to be detail-oriented, and no one is better at fleshing out details than quality assurance employees. The interview should focus on whether the candidates are big-picture thinkers or granular thinkers about how things might work.
- Design—Meeting with Design is more of a soft-skill interview to see whether Design can get along with SEO. Rarely will SEO hires have design talent or designers have SEO talent, so they will need to work together very closely as they build sites and pages.
- Sales—For an SEO hire that is primarily going to be focused on link building, it would be ideal to have someone from sales assess whether the candidate actually has strong sales abilities and instincts. This can be a very short interview—a quick first impression on whether they have the communication abilities to make people act.

TIMING

Since there are a lot of people to meet, the process should be broken into at least four stages.

1. **Recruiter Screen**—A recruiter can ask questions about resume experience and ensure the candidate has the right background to proceed through the hiring process.
2. **Hiring Manager Screen**—The potential manager of the SEO hire should talk to the candidate, either in person or on the phone. Aside from questions about how they will work together, the hiring manager should determine in what way each candidate would help the organization achieve its SEO goal.

3. **On-Site Interview**—Provided the candidate passed the first two stages, they should now be brought on-site to meet with Product, Content, and an engineer.
4. **Second-Round Interview**—If they pass the first three interviews, they should then meet with a second round of interviewers, which should include another engineer, marketing counterparts, Design, and Business-Intelligence.

Stages three and four can come on the same day but, if possible, should be split to save time for both the hiring organization and candidate if there isn't a mutual fit. This gives the first round of interviewers time to circle up and discuss the candidate before forcing them to spend even more time with a company that may not hire them.

The right hire is critical; SEO can end up being responsible for most of a company's revenue. A bad hire is always more costly than not hiring someone, so although this may seem like a lot, the right fit is worth the time.

SEO IS DONE BY HUMANS

Within a Product-Led SEO approach, the people are the most important component. Just like you wouldn't have the wrong person build the key product offering of your company, you shouldn't have someone without deep SEO knowledge lead your SEO efforts.

When done correctly, the Product-Led SEO strategy that you implement will not be just a marketing campaign but the product that brands your company in search results. While, at first, your users will find your product via search channels, if and when it is successful, it will grow by word-of-mouth and direct and referral channels. A successful SEO product will be the key to a large portion of your future business.

A function that is this important absolutely needs the right people. Therefore, my recommendation is that you find the person or people who you can envision owning the future success of your company. Put care and diligence into finding people you can trust for this large task.

Anyone with a modicum of SEO knowledge could conduct an SEO audit or build out a keyword list. However, it takes a unique person to be able to combine customer empathy with creativity layered in SEO knowledge. Success in SEO isn't checking the boxes, and this is particularly true in Product-Led SEO. Look until you find someone with the uncommon traits that will lead to a product found worthy by both search users and search engine crawlers.

Hire someone who can operate beyond the bounds of your typical digital marketer. Hire someone who demonstrates adaptability and creativity. They'll be able to handle anything that comes their way.

CHAPTER FOUR

SEO AND DIGITAL MARKETING

A number of years ago, I partnered with a well-known brand to help them understand why their organic traffic had hit a revenue plateau after many years of double-digit growth. They assumed they were under some sort of algorithmic penalty, or maybe they had broken something technically within their site. With millions of pages translated across dozens of languages, I started digging. I assumed it would be a lengthy effort.

However, within minutes of gaining access to all their performance data, I found the answer to the puzzle. While this organization had the most detailed analytics to dissect every aspect of their millions of dollars in monthly spending on paid marketing, when it came to SEO, they were using reports that revolved around rankings on search engines. The reports they shared with me detailed the number of keywords in positions one, one through five, and top ten on Google. Their total traffic had consistently gone up, but the revenue from the entire channel had flattened.

There's an old business school adage that "What gets measured, gets done," and that is exactly what was happening at this company. The SEO team had a goal of increasing the number of keywords in the top-ten results as well as how many they could also get into the top-five and first positions. As their primary goal, the team strived to get as many top positions as possible—even when the keywords in these positions were completely irrelevant to the business of this company. While the SEO team reported on total revenue, it wasn't the goal.

The reason revenue had plateaued was because even though traffic might have been increasing, none of the team's efforts were directed at anything that might have increased revenue. Somehow, while nearly every other acquisition team in the company (excluding social media, but that is another topic) was focused on revenue, the SEO team was divorced from that goal.

While it is easy to blame the SEO team for pushing in the wrong direction, the real issue was at the executive level. For some inexplicable reason, the Executive team was hung up on the obsolete idea of measuring SEO success by the number of keywords in top positions. They had passed along this goal to the SEO team. And…the SEO team delivered exactly what they were asked to do.

I have seen this exact same scenario play out in companies of all sizes.

THE PRIMARY SUCCESS METRIC FOR SEO

It is amazing to me that anyone would still use rankings as a success metric for an SEO campaign. Rankings are a vanity metric and do not directly, or even indirectly, contribute to the success of a business.

Using a rankings report as the only way to measure SEO progress is as asinine as using a paid-marketing budget total as a metric of success. All a big budget shows is that someone can spend money. A big budget says nothing about whether the effort has been profitable. Rankings exhibit the ability to be ON Google, not whether anyone clicks or buys.

When I first started my career in SEO, the critical metric of success was ranking in search results, and more importantly, true achievement was measured by how many number-one positions one occupied. It did not matter whether those were useful positions or even if anyone clicked. Having the search result ranking was a bragging right.

As an added bonus, Google wasn't the only search engine anyone cared about. Having a top result on MSN.com (the predecessor of Bing) or Yahoo also generated some SEO applause and even a proud pat on the back. But that was a very different era, and it turns out page ranking was never a great indicator of business impact anyway.

CONTRIBUTING TO THE BOTTOM LINE

The primary success metric for SEO is and should always have been the same for every marketing channel: the amount of revenue, leads, visitors, etc., the business needs to be successful.

If every other marketing channel is contributing to the bottom line, or at least the top line, and organic traffic is not, there is an issue that needs to be addressed. Great rankings will be little solace if the business goes under for lack of cash.

Some businesses, especially those with long sales pipelines, may have challenges in tracking revenue or any other business metric back to organic-traffic sources. Organic search traffic will be mostly top-of-funnel in these cases. In the case where revenue can't be measured, the fallback measurement option should be clicks from search engines, but an effort should still be made to determine that the clicks are of value.

Even if it's impossible to definitively determine the sources of business outcomes, the business should still be looking at specific metrics from organic sources of traffic using Google Analytics or similar tracking software. These metrics include engagement rate, bounce rate, pages per visit, and time on site. If the engagement rates are too low to ever lead to a conversion event, there is an issue. High rankings leading to clicks are of no value if they don't result in sales.

Again, keep in mind rankings alone, as a KPI for SEO, is a vanity metric and should never be used in budgeting, financial modeling, or any other important business conversation. SEO should be judged in the same vein as every other marketing channel. If you face challenges measuring SEO by the same KPIs that other channels use due to attribution issues, find other proxies that have business impact that can be measured. In lieu of revenue reporting for SEO, use a metric like lead forms completed, demo requests, or even measure the clicks onto a call-to-action button.

PAID AND ORGANIC CHANNELS WORK TOGETHER

Very often, in conversations about digital marketing, I hear SEO (free search traffic) referred to as the opposite side of the spectrum to search engine marketing (SEM). (SEM, in other words, is paid search marketing.) In this view of digital marketing, SEO and SEM teams are competing with each other for resources and budget. In my opinion, this attitude is limited and counterproductive.

I prefer to view paid and organic as efforts that should be working in concert to achieve the same goal, converting a search engine user into a customer. The user who will click a paid listing and the user who will click an organic listing is essentially the same person. Both of these users signal their intent to a search engine via their search query. In both cases, the search engine will answer that intent with website listings.

Once the results are visible, the user can choose to click either a paid or organic result, and their choice will likely be dependent on which listing meets their specific need the most. For a branded query (a search that contains the name of a brand), the user might click a paid result merely because it was available.

FOCUS ON CORE COMPETENCIES

Since paid and organic searches are both going after the same user, I recommend strategizing each channel's core competencies and having each focus on its strengths. This is not a cage match between search channels with one coming out on top to take all the marketing budget. You need both to be successful.

Use both strategically. Be aware your bias may go either way. You may perceive that organic search is best because it's free, or you may believe paid is best because it's advertising. Resist the temptation to only use one.

Unfortunately for marketers, we live in a competitive world, and sometimes, we have to pay for traffic. Work to make it the right traffic. Likewise, for organic, work to get the right traffic. Free is good, but if people don't click a free listing, it's not worth wishing and praying they will. A little ad spend at the right time can make a big difference.

Advantages of SEM:

- **The bid**—The bid can control the placement, which means when it is important to be at the top of the page, like on a brand listing, you can pay more to be sure you rank.
- **The message can be targeted to the intent**—On an organic page, the page can rank on anything, so the content speaks to the broadest possible audience. However, for paid listings, targeted pages can be created for specific search terms. Even further, targeted ad copy can be used for a query to make sure the user knows exactly why they should click.
- **Paid is (almost) instant**—SEO can take a really long time to kickstart, whereas paid can start working almost as soon as an account is funded.
- **Paid is easier to build**—At some point, an SEO campaign is going to require support from a number of different functions, like Design, Content, Engineering, and Product, just to launch an SEO page. Paid can be done without the need for any cross-functional support since there are tools that allow marketers to build landing pages on demand.

Advantages of SEO:

- **SEO is free**—At some point, paid has to justify its budget. If that justification can't be made, there is no sense in continuing to spend. Organic is free and very low cost to scale.
- **Barrier to entry is far lower**—There are going to many instances where a paid campaign might be too expensive

to even try. But SEO can pave the way and show whether it might be a profitable area to invest. Examples could be new product lines or expanding into new countries.

- **Top of funnel**—Since paid obviously has a cost, it needs to generate conversions and cannot afford to be just an awareness channel. SEO can easily be something that generates awareness or introduces potential users to a brand.
- **Lower cost**—There will inevitably be paid keywords that do drive conversions but end up being too expensive to continue buying. Instead of investing in a losing campaign at a higher spend, SEO can fill in the gap for similar search terms.

PAID AND ORGANIC WORKING IN TANDEM

Understanding the core competencies of each channel can give a great sense of how these channels can work together to convert users into customers. Organic can and should focus on traffic that is less competitive and a lot higher in the funnel. For example, organic search is a better fit for long-tail queries that only have a small handful of searches per month. Organic can also help in the mid-funnel for users who might not yet be ready to click the buy button. They may be willing to take an intermediary step, like joining a webinar or viewing a demo from a sales rep.

Paid should pick up the baton where organic is less targeted. Paid retargeting could follow organic users around the internet and remind them to come back and buy. Additionally, paid could dominate brand placements at a very inexpensive cost in a way that organic never could.

Typically, homepages rank organically on brand queries, but

paid can create specific brand pages that meet a brand intent. An example would be "brand X has the best customer service," or "brand X is better than brand Y."

SOLVING THE PAID VERSUS ORGANIC PROBLEM

Part of why paid and organic search may appear to be opposed to each other is because they are generally housed in different organizational structures and rarely talk to each other. In order to work more effectively, I think Paid and Organic teams should frequently meet to discuss specific challenges. They should work more closely together.

Working together will get the teams to think about how they can solve joint problems. Organic can become aware of paid keywords that may not be converting well enough, and paid can learn about more keywords they should be targeting.

With cooperation, both teams will be more effective at reaching their goals. With more efficient spend, the Paid team will have more budget to go after strategies and keywords that are currently unattainable. Similarly, the Organic team can focus their efforts on converting more people who are just too expensive to chase with paid advertising.

If Paid and Organic teams can collaborate, everyone wins. With a united front, these two powerhouse entities can dominate search in a way no competitor with a disjointed Marketing team could ever beat. Both teams are ultimately driving toward the same goal of increasing the acquisition of customers, focusing on different levels in the same customer-conversion process or funnel.

SEO IN THE CONVERSION FUNNEL

The internet, with its ability to track a customer journey, has allowed us to visualize the sales process as a funnel. At the top of a funnel, there are many potential customer prospects who are just exploring the idea of making a transaction. As these users pass through different touchpoints of engagement, the number of potential customers continues to narrow—hence the funnel visual—until finally, the smallest number represents acquired customers.

SEO often has a budget problem; because it frequently sits higher in the funnel and costs less, it is given far less attention than it deserves. Within Marketing teams, the most attention (both good and bad) is paid to the initiatives that cost significant sums of money. Paid marketing results in frequent executive check-ins, quarterly reviews, detailed reporting, and, of course, an attribution system that can give detailed reporting on the funnel; SEO often doesn't.

When executives care more about expensive efforts, organic-search channels end up with the short end of the stick, both from a resourcing standpoint and in terms of who gets the credit. Everyone has a belief that SEO works and is an overall benefit to the bottom line, but there's not a strong drive to understand exactly how the traffic performs.

Without accurate reporting, executives and SEO teams end up falling back on useless metrics like rankings.

Even worse, a natural consequence occurs when budgets are tight. The channel that "kind of" works will fall behind the channel or channels with deeper visibility. SEO teams are left vulnerable and always strapped for resources. The SEO unit ends up scrambling to prove their efforts are worthwhile instead of being able to keep their heads down and work to keep the company afloat. In a weird twist, the Paid team must only defend their budgets, not their jobs. The SEO team—without the budget—has more existential issues.

I think the root of this issue comes from top-tier leadership keeping their blinders on. CEOs often maintain a fundamental lack of understanding of where SEO fits into the marketing mix.

Unlike other performance channels, which are designed to go direct to conversion, SEO is a hybrid between branding and performance traffic. Judging SEO purely as a brand channel overlooks the tremendous impact it produces for the bottom line. At the same time, SEO can't be viewed as merely a performance channel.

So how should we think about the role of SEO in marketing?

SEO LIVES HIGH IN THE BUYER FUNNEL

By its very nature, SEO will typically live a lot higher in the buyer funnel, and in many cases, users will not have any buying intent whatsoever.

To understand this principle, step out of the narrow vision of being a marketer. Step into the wider thoughts you have when you, yourself, search for something. Anything. Much of your search activity will be purely research and curiosity. Today, you likely queried about weather information, sports scores, and stock prices, and the links have no commercial intent.

On the flip side, organic traffic on the brand name will be a lot lower in the funnel. To be totally clear, however, brand-name traffic is not really even organic traffic. A brand should rank for its own brand name, or something is very wrong and needs to be addressed urgently. A site with the strongest Google penalty will likely not surface for its brand name, but more than likely, the issue is technical rather than a Google issue.

SEO AND THE LONG TAIL

True SEO efforts will bring a site significant visibility on the long tail. Long-tail words are types of words it would be hardly profitable to put paid dollars behind. Simply stated, dollars are not laid on these words because they would take too long to convert or would be too expensive to keep.

As the user moves down the funnel, their queries will skew closer to popular keywords because this is the moment when they might engage with paid advertising.

Once the user gets to the bottom of the funnel and has buyer intent, they are more likely to click a paid ad. These ads are clicked either on the brand name or from retargeting on another site. A last-click-driven attribution system will then give 100 percent of the conversion credit to the paid channel— and completely discount all the organic clicks that happened over the prior time period.

ORGANIC IS AN ASSIST

That last click might be the equivalent of a basketball slam dunk or hockey goal. In sports, a coach wouldn't discount the role of all the other players that set up the perfect sequence for someone to bring the ball or puck home.

In reality, building multi-touch attribution systems is complex and incredibly resource intensive. However, don't use the complexity to shrug off measuring what is likely going to be one of your most valuable acquisition sources. There is still *no excuse* for not having a better view of the performance of the organic channel and *no excuse as to* why you haven't invested more in that channel.

To that end, executives need to be aware of where SEO fits into the funnel and manage expectations accordingly. Investing higher in the funnel will get results further down in the funnel.

To illustrate this with an example, let's look at someone using search to plan a vacation.

The first query might be very general, just to get ideas of where to vacation, what activities are in that location, and the cost.

- As the user moves further down the funnel, they settle on a place to travel.
- Assuming they know the dates they want to travel, they start exploring transportation.
- They also check out their hotel options.

Throughout this entire process, they may have visited many various sites, from local chambers of commerce to review sites, hotel sites, online travel agencies, and aggregators.

As the user finally decides on their options, they are ready to purchase. They search directly for the site where they found the best deal. If a paid ad comes up first, so be it; they are click-ing. In the last-click attribution model most less-sophisticated sites use, all the credit would have gone to that very last click. The potentially months' worth of effort on planning that vaca-tion through various pathways would not have been measured. Instead, whenever possible, every site should be measuring visits using a multi-touch attribution model, which we will discuss below.

In the example above of a user planning a vacation, this could be a potential attribution model where the value of the total conversion is divided in a weighted format to all the user's website "touches." This model is only made possible if every touch is recorded and mapped back to each individual user.

- Organic search visit one—20 percent
- Organic search visit two—20 percent
- Direct visit from mobile device—10 percent
- Paid click on Google ad—50 percent

In this hypothetical model, organic would have received 40 percent of the credit for the ultimate conversion.

However, since a multi-touch attribution model is often techni-cally challenging, it may not always be possible. There may never be a perfect way to attribute organic traffic, but at least with the knowledge of where SEO traffic fits into the marketing mix, a solid integrated marketing strategy can be built. SEO might be the first channel to carry the baton in a long marathon, but the baton can be passed to the performance channel when customers are ready to pull out their credit cards.

REPORTING TOOLS

The primary success metric for SEO should be whatever the business uses to judge any other marketing channel. Therefore, there doesn't need to be a specific SEO tool to prove SEO is working. Either a business has sales, revenue, and leads attributed to an organic channel, or they don't. Having an analytics tool in place to show whether traffic is contributing to the goals of the business is important, but this tool should already be in place for every other channel.

As we said above, ideally, the tool or tools used should use weighted, multichannel attribution. Multichannel attribution is analogous to measuring the performance of a sports team and recognizing the contribution each team member makes toward reaching a goal. Giving credit to just the person who scores discounts the contributions of everyone who handled the ball or even defended the opposing team. Applying this analogy to digital marketing, the ultimate conversion event might happen via a paid ad, but there very well could be many touches from other channels that lead the user to that final event.

However, getting to this ideal attribution model is not as simple as changing a t-shirt. There is a significant amount of effort needed to gather data, build data warehouses that will hold all the important, relevant information, test models, and buy the tools necessary to support the process. The more data gathered, the better the attribution system will be in helping to understand which channels are the most effective.

Even without a full multichannel attribution setup, there should be indicators SEO is driving the business forward. For example, knowing SEO helped convert a user might be impossible, but at a minimum, we should know if it caused the user to subscribe to a social media channel or fill out a lead form.

If tracking micro-conversions is too difficult, a simple analytics report on pages per visit (or bounce rate) will show if visitors to the website are engaged with your site or if they just leave without doing anything.

REPORTING ON EARLY PROGRESS

For brand-new SEO efforts, my favorite solution is Google Search Console. I've talked about it before in this book, but I'll mention it here again for sheer usefulness. It is the only tool that shows queries that a website is receiving impressions on even if the searcher does not click. Google Search Console is like a peek under the hood at Google's own analytics.

I strongly prefer Google Search Console to any SEO tool that makes a best guesstimate on SEO visibility based on the millions of keywords they crawl. Google Search Console is not guessing; these are real words that users type in search to see a site. Using Google Search Console, you can see early progress on SEO. You can even see the pages just getting crawled by Google. Newer pages and sites might not be positioned very highly in Google, but even at lower positions, they will be getting eyeballs from Google's billions of users.

At those low positions, newer pages and sites may not get meaningful clicks, but even so, watch the impression count grow—it's the best early indicator of SEO growth.

THE THREE LEVELS OF SEO PERFORMANCE

While we are talking about different stages of SEO growth, I'll explain how I think about SEO performance. There are three levels.

Impressions

Impressions are the first level of SEO growth. Each eyeball on a URL in Google search is considered an impression. Obviously, at higher search positions, the impression number on a keyword will be higher.

Even at lower positions, there will be users that search deeper into Google and see the website's listing. Impressions are an indication that a website or page is in a consideration set for search. Simply put, growth in this number is positive, and declines are very negative.

.

Clicks

A click is when a user clicks a search result and goes through to your website.

- Google measures how many clicks there were on a specific listing regardless of whether the webpage even loads.
- Short visits will not be picked up by script-based tracking systems.
- The click number may not always match visit data in analytics.
- The click number may not always match what is in an access-log tool.

Clicks are a factor of impressions as well as click-through rate.

As a click-through rate from search improves, the users and clicks will grow without any subsequent change in impressions.

Conversions

Conversions are the final and most important result of SEO traffic. Conversion is how SEO campaigns should be judged. If clicks are arriving at a website from search but not converting, they will not produce revenue. This is when a conversion-rate optimization effort would be beneficial.

Impressions mean a website is on the field, eligible, and ready to play. **Clicks** are hits and progress toward an ultimate goal, but what really counts is the winning that happens from **conversions**. Google Search Console can give you a clear view into at least the first two metrics, which will make planning for and measuring marketing campaigns much easier. We'll discuss the other features of Google Search Console in a little more depth in the Technical SEO chapter.

Keep in mind that when reporting on anything related to a marketing campaign or business as a whole, you'll always want to connect the outcomes to the input. HR is not measured on the quality of sales produced by the employees they hire, and salespeople are not compensated directly based on the performance of the accounting team. Likewise, SEO should not be measured on how well Sales teams close the deals created from organic traffic sources. SEO should be measured on how well organic traffic performs once it arrives on the website. Once you're landing impressions, you should work on clicks, and once you're creating clicks, you work on conversions.

All that is necessary in order to show success at SEO is a set of tools that show the growth of traffic as well as where that traffic goes. Extraneous tools, like keyword research, testing, and crawling tools, are helpful, but they don't truly elucidate the performance of SEO. Each of these tools is slightly different, but generally, they use keyword data pulled from toolbars or ISPs and then scrape the search results for these keywords. They will each have their own proprietary way of making assumptions about the level of traffic a site might get, but these are truly only assumptions.

Even Google Analytics or an internally-built, traffic-logging tool should not be considered completely accurate. Google Analytics uses externally-loaded scripts to track page views and visits. If these scripts are interrupted on page load, the data will be inaccurate. In the opposite vein, internal logging tools will likely overcount visits, as they are less capable of filtering out fake visits and page reloads.

The true performance metric for SEO is, of course, whatever the business is targeting—downloads, users, email addresses, sales, and so on. Measuring the growth of traffic for the sake of the number alone is just as pointless as focusing on search rankings. In most cases, Google Search Console can provide much of what you need by itself.

Ultimately, all the traffic you generate has to have some tie-in to real customers who will be the actual "buyers" (in the broadest sense of the word) of the product. Building toward these buyers requires a deep understanding of exactly who they are.

Even if all the analytical tools you use have gaps and are missing important parts of a user's journey, financial reports never lie. Either a user pays/buys, or they don't. This is the data that you should rely on as you build out your reporting systems. Understand who it is that pays you (or whatever the conversion element might be), and track those people back to the original acquisition source. Those people will be aggregated into the persona buckets that should be your focus.

BUYER PERSONAS FOR KEYWORD RESEARCH

Personas are very popular on Design teams and in various Marketing teams, but so few people actually use them in their daily work life that the investment in building them is hardly worth it. Many times, when companies build out these personas, they go overly deep into developing exactly who these customers might be.

Even worse, when teams actually need real people to help build the use case for their products, they go directly to customer interviews and skip all the persona research. Having been on both the creation and utilization sides of personas, I can completely understand why personas aren't used even when they might make sense.

Personas might be passé, but when it comes to SEO, I recommend that some sort of persona research be the foundation of any good keyword research. Too many people begin the process of keyword research by firing up their favorite keyword tool and picking keywords off the list. They think high monthly search volumes relevant to their business are all they need. Unfortunately, starting with keywords sorted by volume puts the emphasis on the wrong metric and leads to creating content that might not match the intent of a user or the needs of a website. Attracting traffic that won't convert becomes an expensive hobby.

Rather than using comparisons with competitors or building lists of desirable keywords, write for real people who will become actual customers.

It makes the most sense to prioritize exactly the kind of content needed to help a website monetize. Prioritize based on customer need more than any other arbitrary metric.

The easiest way to figure out exactly what content is necessary is to go through a persona exercise to understand exactly how, why, and what users want from the website. Only armed with this knowledge, once the user's needs are taken into account, does it make sense to distill those topics into precise keywords.

Persona research should answer questions, such as where in the buying funnel a user might be when they're visiting a particular piece of content. Funnel location can guide the depth of content a user expects to see. Long pieces of content might be required when users are high in the funnel—the awareness stage—while short snippets are more appropriate at the bottom of the funnel.

It is also important to understand the devices that a user will be using to access the website. Is it a desktop? A mobile device? Or maybe the user can be served with a voice-enabled device. Knowing these precise details can quickly inform the decision of whether long-form or image-heavy content should be used or is even appropriate.

BUILDING SEO PERSONAS

Before embarking on a persona effort, it is worth acknowledging that existing personas likely will not be detailed enough for you to use for SEO. It is not a wasted effort to build specific personas just for SEO, and in fact, I recommend it.

Current company personas are likely to have details that are not necessarily helpful for SEO, like age, gender, and career stage. Unless these characteristics affect how someone might search, they don't actually matter; what matters is search behavior.

With that in mind, here are the best practices for developing personas specifically for SEO.

1. Identify all potential users of a website or product.

Who is your user? Identifying the user of your website, product, or service is where keyword research as the start of an SEO effort typically fails. Just because a website or product exists doesn't mean users will automatically want to search for it.

Take a step back to think about who might be the users of your website. Knowing who your users are, gives you a good foundation for what kind of content and keywords to focus on. For example, an e-commerce website might want to target people with a specific need, and the focus of SEO should be solving that need rather than just optimizing the product page. A software-as-a-service (SaaS) product might have a similar phenomenon. In both cases, targeting the problem rather than the solution will yield more search traffic.

2. Determine how the users might search based on where they are in the funnel.

Again, traditional keyword research would only identify the popular terms for a vertical, not how the targeted users will search. Users very high in a funnel will be searching for a solution to a problem, while users at the very bottom will be looking for the brand plus pricing info. Where are your users, and what do they need at this moment?

3. Slot users into the type of content they might expect.

There is a lot of advice around what kind of content is best for SEO, but none of that advice takes into account the granular needs of a specific user.

If a user is merely searching for a price or a list of features, they will be ill-served by a long-form piece of content. Similarly, a user who wants a product review would not be helped by a quick list of bullet points. What type of content is most helpful for your user at this part of their research?

4. Match the user with a specific call to action relevant to where they are located in the buying funnel.

Search traffic is a means to an end, not the end itself. Even on a media site that targets readership, an increasing user count is of no benefit if the users aren't reading. We need users to do a follow-on engagement action if we are to be successful.

The user's location in a buying funnel should determine the appropriate call to action (CTA) for the content. A reader who is very low in the buying funnel might be looking for a way to contact a salesperson, while a user high in the funnel should be encouraged to read more or maybe subscribe to a mailing list.

When content is written for the user rather than keywords, it becomes a lot easier to have a targeted action for users to take.

5. Classify the types of devices your users will be using to access the content.

While we constantly hear the refrain that the mobile web is dominant, mobile should not necessarily be carried forward into executing all SEO efforts. If mobile was the magic ticket, long-form content would have fallen by the wayside in favor of short, punchy, shareable bits. However, long-form content is doing very well in the right contexts.

Even though nearly every web user has a mobile device, there are some things that will always be done on a desktop. Buying business software or expensive shopping is likely going to involve a bigger screen somewhere in a buying cycle. Write content with relevancy to the buying cycle, with an eye on the screen size the user will potentially be using to access that content.

6. Consider whether the user will need precise language or culture cues for internationalized content.

One last thing for sites that have international audiences. It's critical to know what language the user might expect to see content in and if there are any cultural nuances that should be addressed.

Many people who have never done international marketing might not know it's often okay to have English-only content for an international audience. A global audience does not necessarily expect a translated page, so it is often better to just give them content in English that contains the international details and options they need, such as shipping and currency. However, you should know your users and what they expect. Understanding your users will prevent having to create costly language-specific content unnecessarily.

With these best practices in mind, you will be able to develop SEO-specific personas that will guide keyword research. Keyword research, like everything in SEO, should be targeted to real users, not search engines. Having the persona will help with making decisions about how to serve those real users.

DON'T WORRY ABOUT WHERE YOU SIT

The idea of approaching SEO as a product is not impacted by where the SEO team sits. The SEO people can have a Marketing leader as their manager and still advocate for creating individual personas just for SEO even when there are other personas in use on the Marketing team. They can incorporate the customer empathy that is usually found on Marketing teams and convey that to the engineers and, possibly, Product managers who build out the product offerings. Most importantly, they can take their knowledge of how users search and search engines work to build out products that achieve the dual purpose of high visibility and strong engagement.

Wherever the SEO person (or team) sits, they should have a deeply integrated relationship with functions across the Marketing teams. They should meet regularly with Paid-Marketing teams to understand how these two channels can work together. In addition, the SEO people should be included in meetings where business metrics are discussed. They should be present so their voice on how attribution should be weighted can be heard.

As goals are set for the SEO team, they should not be the same as for other teams. On one hand, revenue goals are often harder to meet from an SEO perspective, but on the other hand, they may be able to tap into a vein of untapped demand. The SEO team should absolutely have a hand in setting whatever goals they must reach.

When SEO professionals are on Product-Management teams, it might be somewhat easier to utilize the resources of engineers to build product offerings, but they will have to make extra effort to coordinate with marketing and collaborate with those teams effectively.

Regardless, if you have the right people on the team, smart business goals, and a good product-market fit, your SEO strategy can be successful no matter where the SEO team sits.

If you and your team are adaptable, you can be successful in any sort of organization.

CHAPTER FIVE

STRATEGIC SEO

One of my favorite SEO projects was the work I did with the Quora Product team in 2014. I was introduced to the team via a mutual friend in a Y Combinator incubator cohort. The team was looking for guidance on how to intentionally accelerate their SEO growth. Up until this effort, they had been generating vast amounts of search traffic. However, they hadn't done anything on purpose; the traffic was a simple byproduct of having a great website with interesting content. All of their growth was somewhat accidental.

As I dug into their data, I uncovered various SEO levers that had been completely neglected. No one had worked with the Product and Engineering teams to build SEO into the website. While there were millions of pages of questions and answers, there was no clear navigable way for Google to discover the entire site. As a result, much of the site was completely unknown to Google. The sign-up strategy was also hindering search engines from seeing content in the first place.

(Note: Many sites fall into a trap with internal linking where their algorithms only surface related pieces of content on a page. These algorithms have a tendency to just reinforce SEO efforts on whatever is popular and never give anything not yet popular a chance at the spotlight. Quora did have related links, but all of it was from popular pieces to other popular pieces.)

By working with the teams to identify SEO principles that could easily be incorporated into the website, we were able to grow organic traffic by nearly 400 percent in a very short amount of time. User sign-ups also grew tremendously.

Somehow, because SEO is considered "free" traffic that just sort of comes to you, there is a misconception that you can just throw things at the wall and see what sticks. While yes, this approach will generate traffic, it is a tragic misuse of resources and should never be considered an actual strategy. Search engines can possibly figure out a site without SEO, but why leave that to chance? Incorporating SEO as a part of the overall site strategy is how the real value is unlocked.

Having valuable content is great, but without a strategy that helps expose it to users and search engines, too much of that content will remain hidden. Despite Quora being one of the best examples of Blue Ocean SEO on the internet, they couldn't realize the true potential of their opportunity until they developed and implemented deliberate SEO.

BLUE OCEAN SEO

In their bestselling book *Blue Ocean Strategy*, authors W. Chan Kim and Renée Mauborgne promote a creative approach to marketing. They compare the differences between companies that compete in known markets with defined boundaries versus those that do not. SEO can have similar dynamics.

THE RED OCEAN

When companies are in a known market space with defined boundaries, this situation is known as a "Red Ocean." In the Red Ocean space, companies need to outperform their competition by differentiating on various points of value, offering, price, and experience. As the market gets more crowded, the competition becomes even more fierce, and profits decline for all players.

THE BLUE OCEAN

In contrast, Blue Oceans are wide open spaces where industries do not yet exist. In this space, demand is created by the companies that enter it first. There is always a substantial profit potential. Within a Blue Ocean, there is no competition, and the market belongs to a single player. As the market matures, others will naturally become aware of the profit potential, and the Blue Ocean could turn red.

Think of the ridesharing industry as a prime example of both a Blue and Red Ocean. While Uber started as a car-service dispatch company, Lyft created a brand-new industry in ridesharing.

With Lyft, people were earning a few dollars to give someone a ride in the same direction they were traveling. Initially, this was a pure Blue Ocean, and Lyft had all the advantages of owning a market. Lyft was able to set prices, determine the rules, and build brand loyalty.

As customer adoption grew and this market expanded, other players—Uber included—decided to jump in. Competition grew incredibly fierce as both companies undercut each other on price and product and may have even used underhanded tactics (allegedly). Aside from Uber, there were other companies seeing the profit potential who dove into this market. Ridesharing became a classic Red Ocean.

RED OCEAN SEO

I think the idea of Blue Oceans versus Red Oceans is appropriate for how to think about the state of SEO and content marketing today.

Too often, SEO strategies begin with keyword research and an approach for how much traffic the site will get by ranking on these keywords. The keyword ideas will typically come from one of the popular keyword-research tools on the market, tools available to anyone. What "available to anyone" means is that, literally, anyone with a browser or a subscription to a keyword-research tool can find these keyword ideas and then write content targeting the listed search-volume keywords. This is a classic Red Ocean.

Content of the Red Ocean type becomes a race to the top (but in reality, it's a race to the bottom) of who can write longer, have more research, build better links, and dominate search.

The focus of Red Ocean SEO isn't really on the user, even though everyone claims to be user-centric. The goal of a Red Ocean SEO strategy is to be valued by Google. The content-creation process begins and ends with keyword research. Yes, it might be written in a tone and quality that's supposedly geared to the end user, but if the content never achieves its predicted ranking dominance, it is deemed a failure. Google is the audience.

BLUE OCEAN SEO

On the other hand, Blue Ocean SEO is the complete opposite. A Blue Ocean-type SEO strategy would begin with a hypothesis about users and their potential demand. There is no keyword research to support the marketing effort, and only customer research can be relied on.

The content is then created completely with the user in mind because the Marketing team knows the users will find the content and appreciate it. The content creation can be written manually, targeting a keyword, or, better yet, built into the product in what I call **Product-Led SEO.**

Obviously, in the early days of the internet, everything was Blue Ocean SEO, as there was no keyword validation. No one could be certain that there would be any marketable search volume for anything in particular on the internet.

Jeff Bezos launched Amazon as a book-selling website because he hypothesized that, while there were dominant brick-and-mortar book retailers, there would be demand for buying books online if the option existed.

At its genesis as a company, there wasn't any keyword-research data available to inform Amazon's SEO efforts. Even so, it managed to make SEO very much a part of its product. Every page on Amazon is a template geared toward optimal SEO based on how the content is featured on the page; yet, not all pages will be visible in the top positions of a search engine results page. Rather than measure itself by individual rankings or pages that are out of its control, Amazon measures its reach in aggregate, which is controlled by improvements in the page templates.

Many of the internet's dominant websites built the demand for their core product offerings. We've discussed many examples: TripAdvisor for hotel reviews, Yelp for restaurants, WebMD for health, and Zillow for home addresses. Before launching their products, there was no way to validate that there would be search volume for any of these categories. Most simply did not exist yet.

With the internet and search, there is most definitely a first-mover advantage, and while all these category leaders now have competitors, they are in a dominant position. For as long as there is an interest in finding hotel reviews or restaurant reviews on search engines, TripAdvisor and Yelp, respectively, will have the upper hand because of their history, brand, and scale of reviews. (Note: The only threat to their dominance is Google's own properties, which is a whole different topic altogether.)

FUTURE BLUE OCEANS

The internet is an infinite sea of possibilities, and there can be Blue Ocean SEO opportunities created in every category. There will be many categories that do not yet exist that will eventually become monoliths of SEO traffic.

To illustrate just a few recent Blue Ocean examples, look at the success of companies like Zapier and Giphy. The core driver of any of these products is NOT keyword-targeted content.

Before Zapier created pages for integrations between two dispa-rate tools, there was no search demand for anything of the sort. The creation of the page fed its own virtuous cycle of demand. Similarly, for Giphy, suddenly, they dominate searches for gifs of every type because we know they have a gif available for almost any occasion.

BLUE OCEANS AND YOU

In this model, successful SEO begins with customer interviews and whiteboards, not on a spreadsheet with search volumes and click curves.

If your research does not find search volume for a particular category, this should not deter you but should rather excite your senses. This means there is an opportunity to create new demand for something in search, provided, of course, there's product-market fit and an opportunity for you to be able to dominate the category.

Identifying your own personal Blue Ocean requires taking a deep look at yourself and your company. Unless you are the inventor of a brand-new product or process, you are likely shar-ing a business offering with many others. Think about why you (or the founders of the company) decided to create the business and why customers should and do choose your business. This is your Blue Ocean—create the content that answers the queries of a user in only the way you can.

If you don't yet know the answers to these questions, talk to your customers or your potential customers. Ask them what is missing in the current offerings for your product or service and how you might be able to fill that void. I strongly believe there is never a point where everything has already been created. There is always an opportunity to do it differently.

If you don't have customers to talk to, go to Quora and Reddit and read the questions people are asking and answering in your business category. Run a survey with a list in your business category, and if you don't have a list, pay people to respond on social media. The best part about using a survey for this purpose is you are engaging with your audience, and they are helping to build your eventual product. By incorporating audience feedback, you'll be that much more likely to succeed.

There are many ideas out there; you just need to unearth them. There is infinite potential in content and user utility, and there will always be something you can create to satisfy users.

Your business and products were created to be different. Embrace that in the way you market them online and the content you create. Create the content that you, and only you, now know there is untapped demand for. Google will reward you and will direct users to you with search-query suggestions. You yourself will actively build the search demand for your offering.

QUERIES AND SEARCH

Initially, Google's core algorithms were focused on ranking its index of websites in an ordered list in relation to a user's query. As the algorithms matured, Google incorporated AI to try to better understand what a user is seeking and help them search better.

With a BERT (Google's neural-learning algorithm) search goal in mind, Google uses a few very visible tools:

I. "DID YOU MEAN"

When Google believes you meant to search for something other than what you typed into the browser, it will suggest another query. Depending on how certain it is of the other query, Google might show the new query's results by default or just give a clickable link to run that new query.

The "did you mean" feature frequently comes up on misspells, but it will also be triggered by other signals, like word combinations or location.

2. GOOGLE SUGGEST

As a user types a query, Google will be one step ahead of the user and try to determine what the user is seeking. The very idea of suggesting a query might push users down certain query funnels they might not have used if they were left to their own devices. As an example, if you typed "best places" into a search box and Google suggested you search for "best places to eat with live music," you might click that option and see results you never meant to search. The source for Google Suggest comes from real-time queries of other users.

Google Suggest is constantly running, and you can see how useful this is just by typing one letter into Google and not hitting enter. The feature was recently dissected in a *Wall Street Journal* investigative report that claimed Google scrubbed Suggest to push people down paths it (Google) wanted them to go. I believe this allegation is highly unlikely in practice, but nonetheless, this feature is tremendously powerful in directing search users.

3. RELATED QUERIES

Very similar to Suggest, Google helps people discover new queries that might better help them find what they seek. Instead of doing Suggest in real time, Google links to other queries that will kick off a new search.

4. "PEOPLE ALSO ASK"

"People also ask" is a new feature in Google's results that both kicks off a new search and (many times) displays a featured snippet response to the question. This is a particularly interesting feature in Google search and highlights the answering feature of search that Google might prefer.

In the early days of search and SEO, websites were very focused on ranking at the top of the results page on specific terms that were assumed to have high monthly search volumes. Due to the immature (at the time) algorithms of search engines, users were trained to only use those big-head terms if they wanted to find useful results.

Today, there are results some in the SEO world consider to be more valuable; these are called "featured snippets." This is when Google takes a portion of a website's content to answer a user's question and puts it in a box in the first position. Ultimately, these featured snippets are giving away content to search users without a need for a user to click a link to the site. If you are just looking for awareness, this might be a feature; otherwise, I try to avoid ending up in these boxes.

BETTER SEARCHING

With all Google's features aimed at getting users to search

better, I would argue the entire idea of a head keyword is obsolete. Generally, super-head terms like "hotel," "car," "restaurant," and similar terms will yield such useless results that Google already modifies them. The results for these queries are based on user location. This means no single website could rank nationally (or globally) on the search terms for all searches.

Additionally, if a user were to search these terms, Google would push them down a more specific path that better matches what they are seeking. I have also noticed all these search suggestions are completely personalized based on my past search behavior.

There was a time when Google personalized search results based on specific user's past searches, but they deemed that to be unsuccessful. Instead, Google uses past search behavior to help a user search better.

Here's an example of a personalized search in the feature "People also ask."

If I search for things to do nearby on a rainy day, Google will help me refine my query with locations I have actually been. When conducting the same query in an incognito window, my suggested locations will be completely different.

The same personalized search applies when using Google Suggest. Suggested queries will change based on:

- Time of day
- Location
- Past search behavior

I have not seen related queries change that much, but that

is likely because related queries are part of a query set. Once Google pushes a user into one query set, the related queries are already relevant for that query and don't need any further personalization.

WHY TALK ABOUT PERSONALIZED SEARCH?

Trying to rank on a single popular head term would likely not work out as intended. Due to the non-specific nature of a search, the users that might click through on such results would likely be tire-kickers rather than actual buyers. General head-term keywords have become much less useful than they once were both because users have become a lot wiser about how to search, and search engines do a better job at getting inside a user's head.

As an example, many years ago, I worked at an automotive-content website, and one of the key terms we targeted was the word "cars." Even at that time, it didn't make sense that there would be people who would begin a search for a new car by typing that single word into a search engine, but we received lots of valuable traffic from that term. Today, this would never be possible.

Google has made so many advancements in search that Google would helpfully suggest modifications to general terms like "cars." It also might simply give the searcher results as if they typed something else in, like "car pictures" or "cars to buy." Google will adjust queries based on what you just searched in a prior query too. A query for "Mercedes Benz" would impact all future car queries (within a session) to be related to Mercedes Benz.

Given this reality, rather than trying to rank on head terms, websites should focus on understanding their users and target the keywords they would search for in reality. A keyword, even one that is assumed to be high volume, will not help you with revenue if your users don't search with it. Therefore, as you develop a strategy, building around keywords rather than users should not be the right choice. You should always target users first.

As you shift the target away from rankings and keywords, you'll also need to look at the competition in a different light.

SEO AND COMPETITIVE TRACKING

Competition and competitors are always a touchy subject in any business strategy. In the offline world, attacking a competitor costs a pretty penny and is very visible. However, online, there are many areas of opportunity to unseat a competitor without breaking a sweat.

In the bucket of fair competition, websites can create and promote head-to-head comparisons, bid on a competitor's brand name, or call out their competitors in their paid marketing. But then there are the dirty tactics too: negative SEO attacks, snitching on competitors to Google, clicking their ads to drive up their marketing costs, or scraping their content. These tactics aside, I think many sites approach competition the wrong way with regard to SEO.

While websites might think of their competitors as those that have similar product offerings to them, make no mistake, for SEO, the competitor is any site targeting the same search terms.

WHO IS THE COMPETITION?

To understand this principle better, think of Wikipedia. Wikipedia is just about everyone's competition, even if Wikipedia isn't selling any products.

Similarly, any other site providing information that might satisfy a user's query intent should be added to the competitive set. All sites in this competitive set should be monitored, or at least observed on occasion, to see how they are growing. Pay attention to your competitor's specific tactics, whether in the content type or technical setup. How, specifically, is that site driving growth?

LEARNING FROM THE COMPETITION

I recommend learning from competitors. If there is something that is working for them, learn how to do it better. If a competitor is generating traffic from a specific query set, but not effectively, you can answer the query's intent and serve the user better than they are. Answering the query's intent is an opportunity to create better content.

Content

In the same vein, if a competitor has created content within a specific topic but left large open gaps in their coverage of the topic, this is an opportunity to do it better. A competitor might have a broad approach that can be better capitalized on with a far narrower strategy. For example, a pest-control product site might be able to beat a competitor by having a detailed how-to on using a product rather than merely general-awareness content.

Links

Observing how and why a competitor receives links is another great strategy for growth. Provided a competitor is accruing links in an above-board fashion, trying to understand the intent behind why someone might link to them can lead to even better ideas on where to find new links for your own site.

(Note: If a competitor is using illegitimate link tactics, it might be reassuring to know they are probably similarly weak in other areas of the business.)

TOOLS

To dig in and learn from competition, I use three primary tools.

I. Google search

Search the competitor's site on Google using site queries (site:domain.com) to see how they come up on Google. Observe how many pages they have, title tags, meta descriptions, rogue pages they probably did not want indexed, images, and their content strategy.

2. Backlink tool

Any backlink tool will suffice. Use this tool to dig into the competitor's backlinks, top keywords driving traffic, recent trends on performance, and any similar sites linking to them that you may not have been aware of before. Popular tools include Ahrefs, SEMRush, Moz, and Majestic.

3. A crawling tool

Any cloud or desktop tool will do, but this is where you really learn about how the site is structured and any deeper understanding you could not find on Google yourself. (Note: Many sites do not appreciate their bandwidth being used by crawlers that are not search engines, so do this at your own risk.) Popular tools include Sitebulb, Screaming Frog, OnCrawl, and DeepCrawl.

For SEO, competition is not a bad thing. In fact, it is innate in how search works. Even if you are the only one that has ever offered your service before, you will eventually face competition. There will never just be one result on Google.

Instead of feeling threatened, use competition to shorten your learning curve and develop better strategies. Competition should be welcomed, not avoided. (That being said, predicting how the competition might react should be an essential part of how you develop your SEO strategies.) An advantage to the fast-moving world of digital is that you and your competitors can pivot very quickly, so take that into account.

It might be cliché, but the best defense is really a good offense. If your strategy is so simple anyone with a keyword-research tool and access to freelance writers can copy it, they will. However, if your strategy is complex, multi-dimensional, focused on a specific customer set, and the result of monumental effort, competition is far less of a concern. The longer it takes you to build your solution, the greater the head start you have over your competitors by the time they notice what you have built.

While building the case for an SEO investment based on yet-unproven data, you should be reassured that the bigger your effort (provided the data is correct), the more likely you will see outsized returns and the longer the time you'll spend at the head of the pack with no competition.

SEO efforts are absolutely an investment, and there are no quick returns. You are building a product that will only begin to show a payoff at the end of a period of time, but once it breaks out, the upward trajectory will continue long into the future. From this aspect, I think there are a lot of parallels to financial investing.

THE COMPOUNDING EFFECT OF SEO

In the world of investing, whether at an exclusive hedge fund or a basic retirement plan, the effect of compounding growth is a bigger driver of returns than anything else. Explained simply, compounding is the idea of earning returns—even small ones—that are then added to the principal. Compounding is generating earnings from earnings.

The longer an investment stays in the market, the more it can earn from the compounding effects of growth. To put this into real numbers, a single $10,000 investment made in the stock market and compounded for thirty years at an average annual rate of return of 10 percent will be worth $174,000!

I believe the same holds true in marketing and especially SEO.

COMPOUNDING MARKETING

Who can ever forget the Old Spice videos responding to celebrities in real time or Airbnb's cross-posting on Craigslist? In truth, while there are dozens of candidates for the greatest marketing campaign of the internet age, there are millions that were duds.

Real user growth happens from doing the unsexy acts of connecting with customers and telling the story of how the product improves the lives of its users. Many customers who are persuaded to buy will buy more/subscribe/pay higher year after year. In addition, these customers will tell others they had a positive experience.

Too often, Marketing leaders search for the magic bullet that will drive 100 percent growth in a single year and neglect improvements that would drive 10 to 20 percent growth in the same time. When they miss their 100 percent bet, they are still at the same base or even lower. If they'd do the unsexy, consistent work, they'd get much further over time.

COMPOUNDING SEO

SEO is the best place to see the effects of compounding within marketing. I have yet to see a graph of any website's traffic that did not continue to edge up year after year UNLESS there had been a cataclysmic event, like a site update or Google penalty. This steady growth happens even if no changes at all were made to the site for years—with a caveat, of course, that the site's content must be in an evergreen space.

What this means is that as a site generates traffic from Google, it continues to accrue the positive signs that will allow it to generate even more traffic as time goes on. Over time, the site will accumulate natural links and good user experiences that will feed into search visibility and broader, deeper indexing.

NEGLECTING COMPOUNDING

The best time to invest in SEO is six months before it's needed, but it is impossible to know when that time has arrived. A little bit of effort now is better than no effort at all.

Admittedly, SEO does take a long time to build a solid base, and while it is growing, it seems so slow. It is hard to justify efforts in SEO when a Paid-Marketing team might be spending huge sums and returning larger, immediate amounts. However, doing the right thing isn't always fun. Without trying to start building out SEO, compounding can never begin.

The best hope for anyone who ignores SEO is that their competitors ignore it, too, because, just like in the financial markets, it's very hard to catch up to those who started earlier unless you are just lucky.

Do you really want to rely on luck?

NOT ALWAYS TIME TO INVEST

One last thing to keep in mind with regard to both SEO and investing is that saving for the future is not always the appropriate advice for every situation. Much like an individual who lacks the financial resources to put food on their table or pay rent should not make their situation even more financially untenable by saving for retirement, SEO investments should not be made by businesses that are close to the edge on survivability.

Make no mistake, every effort in SEO is an investment for a gain in the future. Making that investment comes at the expense of other ways you might want to allocate resources. All decisions should be prioritized by the impact on the business, and depending on where the business stands, it may be unwise to prioritize SEO.

In my opinion, most early-stage companies should not prioritize SEO because they are in a time crunch to reach milestones, and SEO will rarely perform fast enough to aid in that effort. Additionally, early-stage companies are very resource-constrained, and every dollar and hour put into SEO will come at the expense of something else that might have helped the company grow faster.

As a company moves into more stable territory and has a bit more breathing room, this is when you will likely want to consider SEO, but only if SEO is deemed an appropriate channel and is the best course of investment at the time. Considering SEO means deciding the why, how, and what you will build to attract search users. These decisions—just like all other business decisions—require allocating many internal and possibly external resources to building out your plan. Product offerings for SEO should go through the same rigorous vetting process as everything else.

Making hard prioritization decisions for your business might mean SEO never gets prioritized, and that is completely fine. SEO is not a requirement for business success if other channels are working and the business is growing. However, even companies that will never get around to building out an SEO strategy should cover their bases by having a technical architecture that doesn't harm SEO.

In addition, there are basic SEO tactics you should prioritize, as they don't necessarily require an SEO strategy and dedicated resources. As an example, there is no reason not to utilize keywords in title tags and heading tags across your site. If there is not a special project to add in SEO tactics to your site, you should include them in other website-improvement efforts.

STARTING WITH THE RIGHT QUESTIONS

If and when you are ready to put resources behind SEO, having a comprehensive strategy makes sense. Ask yourself the following questions:

- Is there something about your site or business that makes you uniquely able to build this offering for SEO?
- Will it be difficult to copy you because you did more than just use keyword research to create content?
- Are you targeting queries that real humans would actually write?
- Is there a seemingly infinite amount of search growth if you build this product offering without continuously needing to reinvest in content?
- Do you believe you can justify the investment in SEO based on downstream revenue?

If you can answer these questions in the affirmative, this is certainly an SEO strategy worth considering. With your strategy in hand, you now want to make sure you have not neglected SEO tactics.

CHAPTER SIX

TACTICAL SEO

In 2010, I was working at a start-up focused on the automotive space. The big idea was to have a specific website for every single make and model of car produced in the US. Each of the sites would have unique content about that car but would duplicate shared assets (like classified listings) across the entire website portfolio. While the unique content was the highest quality, the ratio of unique to duplicate content was only one to ten.

When Google rolled out the Panda algorithm in February of that year, all the websites were caught in the dragnet, and we saw a 40 percent decline in organic traffic in a single day. For a company that had generated nearly all its users and revenue from organic search, this could have been a fatal blow. Recovering this traffic was a do-or-die imperative for the company.

As this was an algorithmic rather than manual penalty, our reconsideration requests to Google's search-quality team were met with non-answers. The Google search-quality team insisted there was not an actual penalty on the sites that could be removed.

After more information about the Panda update came to light, we determined the real cause of the problem. While we had plenty of valuable, high-quality content, it had been overshadowed by our duplicated lower-quality content. We needed to shed this low-quality content and somehow get Google to, once again, value our high-quality content.

The recovery path from that point forward became one of only tactical and technical SEO. Through the use of canonical tags, directives not to index content, redirects, and outright website removals, we reduced our footprint of one hundred plus websites down to twelve. The twelve remaining websites had vastly reduced content, and anything not deemed to be high enough quality was left on the cutting-room floor.

In August of that year, Google reran the Panda update (at the time, updates were launched on an interval basis rather than in real time), and our efforts were rewarded with a strong recovery. Our network of sites, now just 10 percent of its former size, returned back to generating 90 percent of our pre-penalty traffic. However, we didn't stop there. We kept a rigorous focus on having only quality content. By the time we were done pruning the sites, we only had four websites left. In October, Google reran the update, and this time our aggregate traffic reached 125 percent of its pre-penalty levels. Our strategy of improving the sites with purely technical efforts had been rewarded.

We had a great strategy prior to the Panda penalty, and we had tactics to achieve it. After Panda, our strategy changed, and likewise, we needed to adjust our tactics to achieve it. Oddly enough, our tactics after Panda were to undo a lot of what our prior tactics had been. Just like our efforts before had helped us achieve a lofty traffic goal, our new efforts did the same.

While much of this book advocates for developing an overarching strategy for SEO and not just leaving it to chance, tactics play a huge role in reaching your goals. Strategy alone does not lead to success; it is the tactics that ladder up to the strategy that unlocks the full potential of SEO. Without the strategy, the tactics are just scattershot into a void, and without the tactics, the strategy is a lofty idea that will never be realized. Strategy is important, but so are tactics.

Since search is all about queries written by users, the underpinning of any tactical effort is keywords.

KEYWORDS

In the past, in order to rank in a top position, keywords were chosen using keyword-research tools. Preference was given to exact-match words that had high average monthly search volume, even if those words didn't bring in the right users. The keywords were then used in on-page metadata, spun into content at a high keyword density, and (most significantly) used in anchor text (the words that have the link underneath them) for deliberately-built external links.

To keep track of the rankings for those keywords, SEO specialists had to use a slew of tools whose primary function was to scrape search engines on a weekly, daily, or even hourly basis for the latest rankings. Executives asked to see these reports. Having a huge list of prominent top positions was a key component of an SEO role. Many businesses are still in these dark ages of SEO.

This whole SEO process worked, and then it didn't—because things changed.

It wasn't just one thing that changed—EVERYTHING changed.

For starters, Google became the dominant search engine, if not the only search engine anyone cares about. Google earned this role by rapidly improving the search user's experience, a direct result of rooting out the kinds of practices that made pages rank undeservingly.

These days, manipulating a particular ranking is virtually impossible. Even if one put in the tremendous effort needed to successfully manipulate a ranking, it might all be for naught.

Google now has robotaxis on the road. We should stop pretending Google is the same search engine it was a decade ago. Google doesn't just have a better understanding of what its users want, it has used AI to dramatically change how it values links. This, in my opinion, is the change with the biggest impact on users.

BACKLINKS AND MORE

In the early days of the internet and search, Google differentiated itself from other search engines by focusing on quality signals to determine relevancy for a query. Amazingly, the other engines—and yes, there were lots of other search engines—completely ignored quality and looked at keyword matches to pages in the index, a much less useful approach.

The primary signal Google uses to determine quality is the value of the links that point to a specific page or website. The value passed by those inbound links is calculated by the value of their own links. From Google's perspective, the internet is a true web of pages linking and connecting to each other.

Links are a critical part of Google's ranking algorithms, as a link to a page is a vote of popularity and, at times, contextual relevance. Google's insistence on link quality means a good SEO approach must consider links but in a nuanced way.

LINKING UNDERSTOOD

Google modeled its ranking algorithm after a traditional academic-authority model. An academic paper with a new idea is considered to be more authoritative if it has a large number of citations discussing it. At the same time, the quantity of those citations has to be qualified by the quality of the citations, so a paper cited by a Nobel laureate would be more valuable than one cited by a high school senior.

Moving this model over to the web, Google uses the same sort of calculation. A website that has a link pointing to it from Stanford University would, in theory, be more valuable than one that only has a link from Kaplan University. It's not that Google recognizes Stanford is a highly reputable university with a higher caliber of education than Kaplan because of the Stanford "brand," rather, the fact that Stanford has more authority is based on the higher quality of other websites that link to it compared to those that link to Kaplan.

Furthermore, quality is not created by a website alone. The page giving the link will also have its own authority, which will be determined solely by the search engine. From this perspective, a link from the Kaplan homepage to a website is likely to be more valuable from a link standpoint than a private student's blog on the Stanford domain.

Viewed holistically in this manner, the idea of a .edu or .gov website having more link authority than a .com is completely false. Every domain has to stand on its own within the web, based on its own backlinks. It is likely that an .edu or .gov website will have more link value to share, but there is no guarantee. Just to underscore this point, Google knows that whitehouse. gov is the most valuable US government website not because it is the website of the white house but because it has the highest value of incoming links.

MANUFACTURED LINKING

While Google claims to view hundreds of factors in determining rankings, links have always been a very prominent part of the calculation. On its face, this link-calculation algorithm seems very simple to manipulate. High-value links will pass an extraordinary amount of value and help the linked page rise in search rankings.

As a result, almost from the day Google launched its index, huge economies sprung up to help marketers manipulate their rankings via artificially valuable links. On the cleaner end of things, there were reporters or websites willing to accept compensation in exchange for a link placement, while on the dirtier end, there were botnets designed to hack websites just to place links.

In between these two options, there were brokers that assisted websites in finding the perfect place to purchase a link on a permanent or even temporary basis. Up until 2012, all this link manipulation was remarkably effective. Websites that spent vast sums on link building saw their websites dominate valuable positions on Google. But this is not the way Google had been conceived to work. Websites were not supposed to just be able to spend their way to the top of the rankings when Google really wanted its index to focus on user experience and relevancy.

PENGUIN

In 2012, Google released its Penguin algorithm update, whose sole purpose was to identify manipulative linking schemes and demote the recipients of the links. When possible, Google nuked entire link networks, bringing down sites that linked as well as the sites receiving the links.

For the first few months and even years after Google unveiled this algorithm update, websites were terrified of having their previously undiscovered link-building efforts revealed and suffering a resulting penalty. Sites frantically posted disavow files to Google, disclosing shady links they may have had a role in acquiring. Out of fear, websites even disavowed links proactively that they had nothing to do with. This algorithm update gave rise to the concept of negative SEO, where a malicious person could point dirty links at a website and then watch Google penalize the receiving website. (Note: Google claims this is not possible, but there are many case studies of negative SEO working.)

It has now been many years since this algorithm update, and link-buying activity is once again picking up. Websites have become more confident in their abilities to evade Google and use these links to accelerate their SEO growth. This time around, it is called "guest posts" or "sponsored posts" rather than outright paid links.

GOOGLE IS SMARTER THAN YOU THINK

I strongly believe any effort expended on manufactured linking is wasted time, not because you will be caught by Google, but because the links just don't work. Google is a company driven by machine learning and AI. Outside of search, Google's Waymo (the name of Google's self-driving car division) has driven more autonomous miles than anyone else working on self-driving vehicles. To date, in the 5 million miles driven by Google, we have not heard of any serious injury or fatality caused by Waymo, which means Google has AI good enough to make life-and-death decisions. The challenge of driving a large vehicle on the road safely alongside unpredictable humans is light-years more complex than ranking search results.

Any person with even a few minutes of experience at reviewing backlinks could very quickly identify artificial links. Google's AI, which is better than humans at processing large datasets, can certainly do the same. A human may determine a link is artificial even if it's cleverly hidden because the reviewer might recall seeing a similar pattern in the other links. Google's AI can compare a link to data right there in its database. Additionally, Google's crawlers have greater access to links and patterns than any SEO backlink tool in existence could possibly supply. A website might not get penalized when its artificial links are discovered, but the links themselves will still be discounted from the ranking algorithm. The net result is any resources expended in acquiring the links were completely wasted.

NOFOLLOW VERSUS FOLLOW

Anyone who has ever spent even a few minutes around link building has heard of the idea of "follow" versus "nofollow" links. To understand what a nofollow link really is, it's worth going back into the history of Google a bit. Historically, as webmasters figured out links were important in the Google ranking algorithm, they used every means at their disposal, including creating pure spam on Wikipedia and blog comments, to boost their number of links.

To neutralize the attraction of creating spam just for links, Google developed an attribute called the "nofollow" that allows sites to label a link as not trusted. In theory, this would negate any page rank that might flow from a nofollow site and make the links useless.

Many websites inundated with spam links, including Wikipedia, opted to make all their outgoing links nofollow by default. Sites began using nofollow as a way to sculpt the crawl budget both on and off their webpages. For example, a site may be forced to have a privacy policy, but it doesn't want to be forced to have search engines crawl these pages and flow link equity to the page, so it would make all the privacy-policy links nofollow. Externally, page rank is a two-way street, so a site that wants to hoard all of its page rank would nofollow all its external links.

In practice, nofollow probably never worked the way people thought it did. In repeated tests I ran, as well as tests others have written about, a page linked with a nofollow could still rank highly in search results. Viewed through the lens of Google as an intelligent search engine, this makes a lot of sense. If Google's AI is designed to understand the quality and relevancy of a linked page via the strength of the backlinks, why would Google leave an important key to that puzzle in the hands of a human? Its AI is deliberately developed to make those complicated decisions about which links count in the authority weighting and which do not.

Anyone who has ever tried to get a link placed on Wikipedia

knows how hard it is to get that link accepted due to editing constraints. Even if the link is added, an editor will just come along and remove it if it doesn't belong. Google knows all this, and the knowledge of how hard it is to place that link likely takes preference over the nofollow attribute. In this respect, Google just ignores the nofollow.

Similarly, Google can recognize a well-placed link on any other site that has a nofollow attribute and choose to count it in the link graph just as it can recognize a spammy link that does not have a nofollow attribute. In short, it's very likely there's no real difference between a follow and a nofollow link, so at face value, one should not place much stock in the classification of a link. Links should be viewed holistically in terms of how they might help Google calculate the value of a site and not granularly in terms of what the follow status, domain authority, or anchor text might be.

HOW TO BUILD LINKS THE RIGHT WAY

If links are an important component of SEO and can't be manipulated, this might seem like a dead-end for a website looking to increase rankings. Fortunately, there is a solution.

The most effective way to generate backlinks is to not focus on them at all. Rather than think about creating links from a technical perspective, instead build quality content and products that other websites will want to link to. Attract links instead of acquiring them. Most social media links (Facebook, Twitter, TikTok, etc.) do not count as quality SEO backlinks; however, if you can attract social media shares, it is likely your content is resonating and might also be able to score inbound links. On the flip side, if your content falls flat on social media, where shares are a cheap currency, it is unlikely to generate many backlinks. Fortunately, social media and technical link building are not the only options.

The solution is simple and, actually, one Google recommends: build a brand and take a PR approach. Brands don't build links; they get links.

Brands in Search

Google has been accused of favoring brands in search, and that should be true simply because users favor brands! Just like in a supermarket, we gravitate to the branded products over the nonbranded ones; the exact same dynamic happens on a search-results page. As in the earlier explanation about Stanford and Kaplan, Google doesn't give a brand extra credit for being a brand; rather, it recognizes brands because users and webmasters treat them like brands.

Building a brand on the web is not an easy feat, but the first step is to think like a brand. A brand like Coca-Cola doesn't seek websites to link to it; it knows if it creates well-designed products and refreshing beverages and launches good marketing websites, the media will talk about it. A brand focuses on its core product offering first, and only after its product is perfected does it seek to get attention. A non-brand seeks to get attention so it can one day have a great product. (Once again, we return to the idea of Product-Led SEO. Products must always come first.)

Focus on the Right Goal

Focus on the product and let marketing tell that product's story.

That story will establish the brand and lead to links that will reinforce the brand. This does not have to be done without help. Brands use PR agencies to tell their stories, and any company aspiring to be a brand can do the same. There are amazing PR agencies familiar with SEO that can ensure there are links within promotional campaigns, but the PR is the focus, not the link.

If you are not in a position to hire a PR agency, you can still be successful at generating links. Just do what a PR agency would. Build relationships with journalists, understand what they like to write, and pitch stories.

ATTRACTING LINKS WITH A PR APPROACH

Some of the best link builders I know build their links by using PR methods. They create buzz and attention around their products. As others become aware of the buzzworthy product, links naturally propagate. Media links aren't nearly as hard to get as some make them out to be.

Journalists might not respond to the barrage of requests for links, but they will engage with something that appears to be newsworthy or in line with stories they currently write. If you know someone has written about your competition more than once, you can safely assume they might be interested in your product, too. Your request for attention should come across directly and personally as an attempt to share a story idea with them—not a self-serving attempt to generate a backlink.

Your goal should always be getting attention. You may not score a link from every engagement with a journalist, but if you focus on building a relationship, you are better positioned to get a link from them in the future when there is a fit. Having that relationship can allow you to plant ideas about covering your products or permit you coverage on a well-timed product launch. Remember, for backlink-building success, think PR first, links second.

A PR-BASED EXAMPLE

My most successful link-building effort was conducted without an agency and only cost $500. In 2015, I was leading Asia-Pacific (APAC) marketing for SurveyMonkey based out of Singapore. I initiated a partnership with an organization called the Restroom Association of Singapore to run their annual survey. The organization wanted to find out how clean people thought restrooms in Singapore were.

Using Facebook, we targeted a cross-section of people in Singapore to complete the survey. For a total of $500, we received hundreds of responses. As the organization requested, we gained a good sense of where the cleanest bathrooms were in the city, but we also found out how often people washed their hands, dropped phones in toilets, and other similarly humorous tidbits.

We translated our survey responses into an infographic and then reached out to our network of journalists. Not surprisingly, everyone wanted to cover our results. We ended up getting links and mentions in all local online and on-air media. Additionally, we were linked and covered in global media like Yahoo! News and Mashable. Since we owned the data and asset being shared, I was able to dictate how and where the links would go in exchange for a license to use the data and images.

This effort was successful for a number of reasons that can easily be replicated in any link-building effort.

1. I partnered with a credible organization, so even if the data was somewhat silly, there was a respectable organization that put its name on it. Whatever vertical you are in, there is likely an organization that will partner with you to benefit from free advertising.
2. The data was interesting and unique. I had not repackaged anything anyone had ever seen before. This was my survey, and I was able to make it interesting enough to publish. In your link-building efforts, be creative and generate unique data.
3. The data was interesting and link-worthy. Whatever vertical you are in, try to think outside your bubble to come up with something the media might want to write about.

Links are and always will be a part of the ranking algorithm. However, it's best to think of the algorithm like the smart human Google intends it to one day be. If a human could easily detect an unnatural link, the algorithm likely can too. Instead of using precious resources to build unnatural links, deploy that effort to earn natural ones. A clever infographic, a media campaign, a billboard, or a unique approach to data can all be used to generate the buzz that leads to links.

Don't focus on building links by any means. Instead, view links as the byproduct of brand building that Google always intended them to be. Links are just a piece of the algorithm designed to inform Google about authority that should already exist.

INTERNAL LINKING

The authority lent by an inbound link doesn't just apply to external sites linking in; the same applies to internal links (pages within a site), too. A website draws its overall authority score (PageRank, as Google's ranking patents refers to it) from the sum of all of the authority of sites that link into the site.

The best way of explaining this is to use the words from Sergey Brin and Larry Page's original research:

> Academic citation literature has been applied to the web, largely by counting citations or backlinks to a given page. This gives some approximation of a page's importance or quality. PageRank extends this idea by not counting links from all pages equally, and by normalizing by the number of links on a page. PageRank is defined as follows:
>
> We assume page A has pages T1...Tn which point to it (i.e., are citations). The parameter d is a damping factor which can be set between 0 and 1. We usually set d to 0.85. There are more details about d in the next section. Also, C(A) is defined as the number of links going out of page A. The PageRank of page A is given as follows:
>
> $$PR(A) = (1-d) + d \,(PR(T1)/C(T1) + \ldots + PR(Tn)/C(Tn))$$
>
> Note that the PageRanks form a probability distribution over web pages, so the sum of all web pages' PageRanks will be one.[2]

In layman's terms, this is just saying each page begins with a

---

2   Sergey Brin and Larry Page, "The Anatomy of a Large-Scale Hypertextual Web Search Engine," *Computer Networks and ISDN Systems* 30, no. 1–7 (1998): 107–117.

score of 1, and its final score is a function of all its outbound links added to the score of all its inbound links.

In this calculation, the most-linked page on a website will tend to be its homepage, which can distribute the site's authority throughout the rest of the website through its own links. Pages close to the homepage or linked-to more frequently from pages linked from the homepage will score higher. In this regard, achieving the right mix via internal linking is critical.

INBOUND LINK AUTHORITY

Additionally, the homepage will never be the only page that receives authoritative external links. If an internal page is the recipient of a powerful external link but doesn't link to other pages, that external link is essentially wasted. When pages link to each other, the authority of all external links is funneled around a site to the overall benefit of all pages.

For sites with flat architecture or only a handful of pages, a proper internal-link structure is simple and straightforward. On large sites, improving the internal-link structure can be as powerful as acquiring authoritative external links in terms of its impact on SEO. (A large site, in this case, might be one that has as few as one hundred pages.)

LARGE SITE CHALLENGES

An orphaned page is defined as a page that doesn't have any or many links pointing to it. Due to the nature of how many large sites are structured, there are invariably going to be orphaned pages. Even a media site, like a blog or daily news site, that has very clean architecture will have an internal-linking challenge.

A daily news site or blog already has each post/article living under a specific day, which helps with daily organic traffic. However, more than likely, the site will desire organic traffic that isn't just someone searching something related to a specific date or timeframe. There will be posts it might hope will be highly visible many years into the future. Think of the review of a product on its launch day. That review will be relevant as long as the product is on the shelf. Or think of a well-researched item that explains how something works, for example, the electoral college. Granted, these posts were published on a certain day, but they are relevant for many queries essentially forever.

How, then, should we approach the link architecture for SEO purposes?

IDEAL LINK ARCHITECTURE

As you might imagine, for all sites with this challenge, creating an ideal link architecture that flows links around the site can have a huge impact on overall traffic as these orphaned or weakly-linked pages join the internal-site-link web and gain authority.

HOW TO IMPROVE THE LINK GRAPH

Build related page modules on each page that have algorithms that search across all pages with similar content and display related links. Sometimes, when these algorithms are developed, they key off specific connections between pages. This has the effect of creating heavy internal linking between popular topics while still leaving pages orphaned or near-orphaned.

There are three possible ways to overcome this effect:

- Add a set of random links into the algorithm and either hard code these random offerings into the page or refresh the set of random pages whenever the cache updates. Updating this random list of links every time the page is requested might be resource-intensive, so you can achieve this outcome by just refreshing this list once per day.
- In addition to related pages, include a linking module for "interesting" content—which is driven by pure randomization—refreshed as in the first recommendation.
- Include a module on every page for the most recent content that ensures older pages are linking into newer pages.

As an aside, I always like to build an HTML sitemap for large sites, as this gives one place that every single page is linked. (Many years ago, Google had a limit on how many links could be on a page, but that limit no longer exists, so there is no downside.) If the sitemap is linked in the footer, it will achieve the goal of having most pages just one click from the homepage. While Google has suggested HTML sitemaps aren't necessary, I have always found them very powerful on large sites. For example, I worked with a major content brand that was experiencing slowing growth despite an influx of hundreds of thousands of new pages via an acquisition. After a deep-dive technical audit, my only finding was that internal links were lacking. After implementing a comprehensive site directory, they began seeing steep growth, most of which came from the discovery of these newer pages. A site directory does not have to be a visually well-designed page to be effective. It can truly be an alphabetized list of every category and page on a website.

VISUALIZING INTERNAL LINK GRAPHS

To visualize what a desired structure of internal linking should be, I tend to think of a site's link graph like an airline route map.

Singapore Airlines

The least effective internal-link graph looks like the route map of a national carrier for a small country. These air carriers will have a single hub in their capital city and spokes pointing around the world from that hub. Think of the route map for Singapore airlines, which has impressive reach for a flag carrier, but with only a few exceptions, all its flights terminate in Singapore. Applying this mental visual to websites, think of the hub as the homepage. The homepage links out to all the other pages, but very few of the internal pages link to other pages. In order for the search crawler to discover a new page, it would have to first visit the homepage.

United Airlines

The most common type of link graph looks like the route map of a large, global carrier. Think of United Airlines as an example. There are very clear hubs (San Francisco, Los Angeles, Chicago, Newark, Houston, Denver, etc.), and these hubs connect to each other and other smaller satellite cities. Again, applying this visual to websites, the homepage would be the biggest city on the route map, for example, Newark, which links to all the other big cities in addition to all the hubs. The other hubs would be important category pages, with a lot of inbound links and links out to all the other smaller pages. In this link graph, important but smaller pages would only have one pathway to get to them. (As an example, Mumbai is only connected to Newark.)

Search crawlers will only discover new pages if they are linked from one of those hub pages, and the crawler will not find that new page until it revisits the hub pages.

However, the ideal internal-link graph looks like the route map of a budget airline that thrives on point-to-point connections. To the bicoastal business traveler, this route map makes no sense, but the wandering tourist can get to anywhere they need to go as long as they can handle many stopovers. Southwest Airlines is a great example of this structure.

Southwest Airlines

Southwest has such a complicated route map; it doesn't even show it on its website. You would have to choose a particular city to see all the places you can get to directly. There are certainly some more popular cities within its route map, but its direct flights almost seem to be random. A traveler can fly directly from Cleveland to major travel gateways like Atlanta, Chicago, and Dallas, but they can also go to Nashville, St. Louis, Tampa, and Milwaukee.

This is how a website should be structured. Pages should link to important pages but also to other pages that seem to be random. And those pages should link back to important pages and to other random pages. Wherever a crawler enters, it will eventually find that new page, as there many pathways to get there.

To summarize, think of a search engine crawler passing from one page to another, calculating authority as a traveler intent on flying to every city on an airline's route map without ever needing to go to a single city more than once.

On Singapore Airlines, a traveler could get from Mumbai to

Frankfurt via Singapore, but to get from Frankfurt to Paris (without a codeshare), they would need to go back to Singapore. Despite the relative closeness of Paris and Frankfurt, the traveler still needs to go back to the hub to make that connection. The hub limits the ability to get from one place to another directly.

On United Airlines, a traveler could get from Portland to Dallas via Denver and then go on to Fort Lauderdale via Houston. They would certainly make it to a number of cities, but at some point, they would find themselves connecting through Houston or Denver again. The major stops happen over and over again.

On Southwest Airlines, a traveler could begin their journey in Boise, Idaho, on any one of the ten non-stop flights flying from there and make it to nearly every city on Southwest's route without ever needing to repeat a city.

While the focus of this section is on internal linking, the Southwest Airlines structure is also an ideal way to flow link value from externally acquired links. Since every page is connected in a web, each external link will benefit multiple pages no matter which page the link is directed at. Build your internal-link architecture like the Southwest Airlines route map, and you will never have an orphaned or sub-optimally linked page again. In addition to the effective flow of search crawlers, your site will be best positioned to maximize the crawl budget it is afforded by search engine crawlers.

A LOGICAL UNDERSTANDING OF CRAWL BUDGET

The phrase "crawl budget" is an SEO term frequently included in discussions about technical SEO, but it is typically used incorrectly. Most of the time, when people refer to crawl budget, they are considering it a technical SEO enhancement to improve the way Google understands a website. In fact, it is far simpler than that.

The best way of understanding various aspects of Google's algorithms is to view them from a financial standpoint. Crawling and indexing the web is a very expensive proposition. Google was able to beat out every search engine to dominance because they figured out how to do that before the money ran out. While it would be ideal for Google's crawlers to simply gobble up the entire web in one fell swoop, that would be technically impossible. Crawlers need to literally crawl through the web, discovering link after link. As they land on a page, they build a copy of that page into their database.

In the early days of search, while Google was still living on venture-capital money, the engineers needed to come up with a way to efficiently crawl the web without going broke in the process. They came up with a system that decided how much "budget" each site was allocated based on its importance to Google and the web as a whole. That is crawl budget.

If a site is very important to the ecosystem, Wikipedia, for example, Google would have wanted to allocate a lot of its hypothetical dollars to crawling as much of the site as it could. Alternatively, a brand-new website with no authority on the web would be allocated a significantly smaller amount of budget.

This all makes logical sense. Taking this logic one step further, if a brand-new website had thousands of pages, but only a few of them were valuable, it would have been very likely Google's budget would have been eaten up by the crawler ingesting the lower-quality pages without ever seeing the good ones.

The best approach for a website in this position is to simply block the lower-quality pages from search engine crawlers.

To illustrate this with an example, think of a website like a Happy Meal with a toy inside. You have a certain amount of daily budget to buy Happy Meals, but you want a set of unique toys to complete a series. The only way you could find out whether the toy in a particular Happy Meal is the part of the set you still need is by buying the meal and opening the box. So, every time a Happy Meal is bought and a duplicate toy shows up, that day's budget is wasted (unless you were very hungry). The most efficient way to collect toys would be for McDonald's to show the name of the toy on the outside of the box, and then you would choose only the box you wanted.

Continuing this Happy Meal-to-website analogy, those no-index directives and canonical tags are the best way of informing a search engine to ignore a particular box. The crawler then has more awareness of how to most efficiently spend its limited budget.

The idea of crawl budget applies to every website on the web regardless of authority. However, more authoritative websites typically have more budget to be expended by the crawler. As a website gains authority, likely via links or other user-engagement signals, its budget will expand. Google sets the budget; without user engagement, there is no other way to get more budget.

Google refers to this as "crawl demand," and while they don't specifically mention authority in their blog post on crawl budget, they sort of tiptoe around it by calling it "popularity."

> Even if the crawl rate limit isn't reached, if there's no demand from indexing, there will be low activity from Googlebot [Google's web-crawler software]. The two factors that play a significant role in determining crawl demand are:
>
> - Popularity: URLs that are more popular on the Internet tend to be crawled more often to keep them fresher in our index.
> - Staleness: our systems attempt to prevent URLs from becoming stale in the index.[3]

This idea of the budget was a key component of Google's crawling algorithm, and it still exists today. (Though the budget is vastly expanded.) Google now has lots more money and resources to crawl the web, but the web is also bigger and more complicated.

One other change is that budget was likely initially calculated in small amounts of kilobytes, which equated to a number of pages. If a site has dynamic scripts that are more expensive for the crawler to run, a crawl budget can be eaten much faster.

While the actual budget allocated to a specific site will always be a secret known only to Google, Google shares some of its data in your Google Search Console. In 2020, Google launched a new crawling report in Google Search Console that allows users to understand errors Google discovers as it crawls a site.

---

3   Gary, Crawling and Indexing Teams, "What Crawl Budget Means for Googlebot," *Google Search Central Blog*, Google Developers, January 16, 2017, https://developers.google.com/search/blog/2017/01/what-crawl-budget-means-for-googlebot.

This is a very helpful report and should be referenced anytime there are crawl-budget concerns.

A DEEPER LOOK AT GOOGLE SEARCH CONSOLE

We've briefly discussed Google Search Console before, but while we're discussing technical SEO, let's discuss its other, more advanced features. There are many SEO tools on the market, but most use conjecture and assumptions on how Google might interpret a site. Google Search Console is the only tool that does not have this limitation. There are, of course, many naysayers who claim Google Search Console has its own accuracy issues, but there are certainly advantages to having semi-accurate data from the real source rather than complete guesses.

While I use many tools and try to merge the different data points together, Google Search Console is my favorite and the one I always rely on when there are conflicts. To emphasize some examples of conflicts and data integrity, here are some key benefits to Google Search Console:

1. **Impression data**—The monthly impression data for any particular keyword visible on the first page (meaning all people who search that keyword will see the website). This is the best source of keyword-research data in the world. I have worked with renowned brands whose brand names were the biggest query in a vertical, and in every case, Google had an impression count that was many times the monthly volume showed by any keyword tool.
2. **Keyword visibility**—If Google Search Console says your website was visible for a query, it was visible for a query. It really does not matter if any other SEO tool says you are not visible for a query.

3. **Traffic trends**—In many instances, I have had clients be concerned about traffic changes for theirs or a competitor's site in an SEO tool. If that same trend is not visible in Google Search Console, it is not real, and the traffic change in the SEO tool is likely a result of calculating visibility on keywords that might not actually matter. Likewise, if you see a traffic change in Google Search Console, you should trust it, even if an SEO tool told you everything was smooth sailing.

With this in mind, here are the top utilities you can get out of Google Search Console.

1. **Coverage**—There are many gaps in the coverage reporting in Google Search Console, but it is the only source that knows how many pages of a website are included in Google's index. Conversely, when pages are being dropped out of the index from an error or other issue, this is the place to find out what happened.

2. **URL lookups**—On a URL-by-URL basis, Google Search Console has the option to see whether a URL is indexed and whether Google accepts a canonical suggestion. (Canonical directives allow websites to suggest a canonical or primary-source page when there is a duplicate page.) You can even see how the page was rendered by the crawler.

3. **Data comparisons**—There are now many months of data in Google Search Console, so there are many possible comparisons you can make. For example, traffic can be compared year over year or week over week, and you can even drill into specific URLs and queries.

4. **Filtering**—Filtering leads into one of the best primary features of Google Search Console. You can compare sets of URLs, keywords, devices, countries, and many more options.

You no longer need to just trust aggregated charts—you can dig into the numbers behind the graphs yourself.

With the information and filtering capabilities of Google Search Console, you are able to filter and find anomalies that are either worth investing in or currently hurting the website. Anytime I see large movements in traffic, the first thing I will do is start comparing present dates to prior dates (either an immediate previous date like last week or a year earlier for more entrenched websites). You can then sort this data by greatest difference, either positive or negative. The insights you will find should give you a direction to continue digging. This might include filtering for URL, country, device type, or specific date.

If you find a problematic URL, you can look at it in the URL look-up tool to see if there was a particularly troubling change on that URL. Some of the things you might see are errors related to indexation, canonicals, or loading the page. If you don't have any errors, it is time to start using other forensic research to track down what might have changed on the page or on the website as a whole.

This sort of forensic analysis can be very granular, but it also might be the only way you are going to find specific issues that might have occurred on a URL or keyword. Looking at general trends will not give you any specific guidance on what might have gone off the rails.

HERE ARE SOME IMPORTANT THINGS TO LOOK AT IN GOOGLE SEARCH CONSOLE.

1. Brand versus non-brand

Many people assume they are doing well in SEO based on

looking at the total number of organic visits coming to their site; however, what they may miss is that much of this could just be branded traffic.

Brand traffic is great, but it doesn't indicate SEO success. The click for brand arrived organically. The user clicked through from Google rather than directly typing the domain name into their browser.

Growth of branded traffic will plateau at the natural penetration level of the brand. Branded SEO traffic will only grow at the rate a brand expands its awareness. On the other hand, non-brand traffic can grow infinitely if a company continues to imbue creativity into its SEO efforts.

Knowing the ratio of brand to non-brand traffic is critical when assessing the current progress of SEO efforts. For companies that have not yet invested in SEO, it's not unreasonable for their brand versus non-brand ratio to be 90/10. A company that has a smaller brand footprint and has invested in SEO for many years might be closer to 20/80.

When I first joined SurveyMonkey, branded traffic was close to 90 percent. Through years of effort at creating Product-Led SEO and building out a global strategy, by the time I left the company, this ratio was better than most pure-content websites that do not have a strong brand.

2. Comparison report

Using the comparison tool, it's important to do frequent year-over-year checks on important pages to ensure they are continuing to accrue more traffic than the prior year.

Checks for year-over-year stats should be done for brand and other important queries as well. There may not always be something to do about the information (yet), but it's important to at least know it.

3. Canonicals

As a canonical link is only a suggestion to Google, knowing whether those suggestions have been accepted by Google is very useful information. It is helpful to sort through URLs receiving traffic to ensure they match the expected URLs and note if there is a canonical issue.

4. Errors

Unfortunately, there are many errors that Google Search Console reports on that aren't really concerning. However, there are always issues worth addressing. The Google Search Console team has said they will clean up the reporting here, but some errors that are important are schema, crawling, and definitely anything related to robot files. If you find an error that is fixable, for example, missing schema (technical markup that allows you to describe features or products in structured data) or a page that is blocked to search crawlers, that is certainly something worth addressing immediately.

When it comes to any technical SEO research, Google Search Console should be considered the absolute word of truth. The visibility that Google shares there is the only accurate source of a site's true visibility. It is as if Google is sharing their own internal analytics on Google search behavior for your queries. One area where Google Search Console can be particularly helpful is in identifying problems with duplicate content.

DUPLICATE CONTENT

When people sit around thinking that Google is out to get them, they discuss the popular idea of a duplicate-content penalty. As a result, there is a level of unjustified paranoia around ensuring all content is unique. People make huge efforts to spin duplicate content into something else. There is even an obsession with blocking pages to Google's crawlers if content is not unique.

In fact, duplicate content is an issue, but there is no actual penalty applied to anything that is deemed to be duplicate. From a user perspective, Google wants to make sure all content in a search result is completely unique to other results, so a user doesn't see a results page with seven to ten listings of the exact same content. This could be content from the same site or even across different sites.

Therefore, when Google identifies duplicate content, it has an algorithm that determines the canonical version (the word for "primary" in the search engine lexicon) of that content. In its analysis, it will take into account any canonical directives in the source code, but there is no guarantee it will agree with the site's assessment of canonical. As Google determines its own assessment of canonical levels of content, it looks for authority, user experience, and what algorithmically seems like the best overall fit.

Provided the content is not a doorway page intended to trick Google into ranking a page undeserving of being ranked, duplicate content is not harmful.

Having duplicate content on a site is usually not an issue that could hurt a website, and it should not be avoided. The exception to this rule is if an entire website is duplicated from another site or so much of a website is duplicate, it could fall into the realm where the Panda algorithm might think the website is of too low quality to be included in Google's index. Duplicate content can come in many forms, and in many cases, it can be very valuable for users. For example, product descriptions are usually sourced from manufacturers and are duplicated across all websites that sell that product. There is no reason to avoid hosting this content or go through the extra effort of changing a few words to make the content unique.

As another example, wire news services like the Associated Press or Reuters have their news syndicated across many media sites. If a website such as CNN.com or the *New York Times* did not include this content, it would be doing its users a disservice.

When it comes to how Google ranks this duplicate content in both of these examples, it will choose the website that best matches the user's query and allow the duplicate content to rank on the query. Depending on the query, a user may see a product page on Amazon, while another user would see Walmart.com in the first position for the same query. Query modifiers like "near me," "reviews," or "free shipping" could be determinants that drive visibility. On that same note, there is no hard rule on whether websites should make duplicates of their pages for every city or state they service. The answer to this is specific to each site, but as long as there is no manipulative intent, it is likely an allowable strategy.

In short, duplicate content, if it otherwise fits the overall purpose of a website and was created to be useful for users, does not need to be avoided. As with everything related to SEO, the overarching principle should be whether something is good for users. Anything that meets that bar is perfectly safe to use.

One area that is a common source of duplicate content is the lingering legacy of site moves and updates. So, when undertaking any big update or migration, it is vital to get it right.

SITE UPDATES AND MIGRATIONS

Much like any offline business that likes to refresh the paint, reorganize a storefront, or renovate, online businesses or company web presences tend to get refreshed periodically. However, when reconfiguring an online presence, there is a lot more that must be considered when it comes to SEO.

Choosing a new technology vendor, folder structure, or just a homepage update will most likely have an impact on the way Google and other search engines perceive a site. This isn't to say that change should be avoided at all costs; rather, certain precautions should be included in any change plan.

The biggest concern when updating a site is that search engines will no longer be able to find the old pages where they used to be and also have a hard time finding the new pages. This will have a double impact of lost visibility on old pages and not recovering that visibility on new pages. Therefore, the goal in any update is to maintain the structure of the old and nimbly pass users and crawlers on to the new.

The best practice to achieve this goal is to set up permanent redirects from the old page location to the new URL. Technically, this is referred to as a 301 redirect, which will force browsers as well as crawlers to update the cache for the new URL. (This is in contrast to a 302 redirect, which is considered to be just a temporary redirect.) Temporary redirects are useful in passing users to a new URL as a result of a particular state (login cookie, time-based, location), but the primary URL still remains the same in the memories of a browser and search engine. We want the redirect to be permanent after a site refresh.

Due to the technical complexities that often arise with a permanent redirect, a temporary redirect ends up being the default redirect option in many popular content management system (CMS) tools. As a result, setting up a permanent redirect must be a deliberate exercise.

In theory, a solid permanent redirect will also pass forward the earned equity acquired from external sites as well as internal links that are used to link to the URL. A successful permanent redirect should help pass forward users as well as authority.

STEPS TO AVOID BREAKING REDIRECTS

Even with best practices followed to the letter, there will inevitably be complications with the redirects. Many of these issues stem from missed redirects that end up as broken pages. The surest way to avoid missing any pages is to have a comprehensive list of every URL on a site placed in a row on a spreadsheet and, in a parallel column, a row with the new URL location.

Since the redirect file will not be a one-to-one, old-to-new map and will likely use algorithmic rules on redirection, pages can still be missed. Before launching the new build of a website, the entire site should be crawled, and it should be verified the old URLs are correctly redirected to new URLs.

Even with the best-laid plans, there can still be issues with how redirection plays out. When a redirect instruction is given to a search engine, the engine is being requested to consider the new URL as equal to the old URL. In practice, that decision is completely up to the search engine.

As the redirect is a change being introduced to the search engine, it is possible the request is not adopted, and the previous authority is not passed to the new URL. This is a not-insignificant risk, and therefore, complete site restructures and site migrations should not be taken lightly. A full site migration should only be undertaken when absolutely necessary for legal purposes or branding needs. In these instances, the primary business need will overshadow the potential traffic and authority loss that could come from a migration. If the business need does not trump a migration that leads to a loss in traffic, alternative plans should be considered.

I have overseen redirects that managed to maintain traffic to a new location exactly as it was before, but I have also worked on projects where there was a 50 percent plus loss in traffic after the redirect. There is no real way to know whether the redirect will be accepted until it is rolled out.

Even redirects within a site have the potential to cause unfavorable adjustments in rankings. A full-site re-architecture should be undertaken carefully, if at all. Again, if traffic loss is an unacceptable cost to an overarching business need, alternatives should be found. An option in this scenario is to use a staged approach, where parts of the site are redirected and, once traffic has stabilized, the next tranche of the site is redirected. This process can continue tranche by tranche until the full site has been updated.

One major consideration to keep in mind with all redirects is the redirects likely have to be maintained in perpetuity. For as long as there are backlinks or users who might find the old URL, the redirects have to remain in place to avoid sending users and search crawlers to the wrong location.

It is best practice to proceed cautiously when doing redirects and maintain the redirect mapping forever. I recommend you follow these practices in any scenario where URLs are changing, including a site update that just moves a handful of pages.

Even with all the associated risks, change should not be avoided out of fear. Even if there are temporary drops in traffic, traffic may recover slowly, or there may be even more substantial growth in traffic due to a better site structure. The primary takeaway on updates and migrations is that they should be done carefully, slowly, strategically, and with full consideration of the risks.

While it is obvious to most leaders that strategic SEO needs executive buy-in, the need to understand tactical SEO might not be as clear. Even if you are an executive who will never touch a line of code, understanding the wider implications of strategic directives at the tactical level is critical to decision-making. Key terminology, such as linking, structure, crawl budget, duplicate content, and migrations, should make their way into larger discussions of broad organizational decisions and even the lexicon used in internal communications.

I have worked with teams that had specific goals around linking or even crawl budget that were conveyed to them by executives who possibly did not have a deep enough understanding of the recommendations they were making.

Likewise, on crawl budgets, duplicate content, and migrations,

I have worked with teams that lived in fear of the implications of all three of these ideas. When they understood them better, they were able to make better decisions. Most of this book has approached SEO from a manager's position rather than a tactical perspective, but I think a deep knowledge of the tactics and why they work is required for everyone's strategic understanding.

Let's turn our attention to another arena where understanding leads to better decisions: SEO categories.

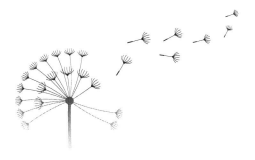

CHAPTER SEVEN

BROAD SEO CATEGORIES

As a result of my role at SurveyMonkey, which is an SaaS (Software as a Service) company, I have, for many years, been approached by founders and leaders of SaaS companies with questions about SEO. Particularly with high-ticket SaaS business-to-business (B2B) products, the prospect of building out an SEO channel is quite tantalizing. Where many SaaS companies typically have to spend thousands of dollars to attract prospects through a variety of channels, the idea of having a search channel where prospects just walk in the door on their own is too attractive to pass up.

When I embarked on my first effort to help an SaaS B2B company with its SEO, I was also under the illusion that this was going to be a supremely profitable channel. I was eventually confronted with a wall of reality that I then needed to convey to a disappointed client. The fact was that an SaaS product sold to a very specific niche B2B audience was not going to create any more demand for its tool by improving on SEO best practices. It would create more visibility within the audience that was already looking for it or its competitors, but that extra few percent of visibility didn't amount to the smashing success everyone had hoped for.

Also, because this product had a very long sales cycle, the few percent of SEO growth wasn't even plainly obvious in the revenue numbers. Due to the high-ticket nature of its product, SEO was likely profitable for this company. The only real question was when there were other places to spend its money, did investing in SEO make the most sense? In the end, we determined there were other, better options.

The key lesson I took from this experience is that SEO is an optimization channel, not a demand-creation channel. SEO efforts improve the visibility of a website when the demand is already there. In a defined niche, there could be very narrow demand that will see significant growth of organic traffic when the site is first optimized for search, but then it will only grow at the rate of demand growth for the product and brand.

Over the next few pages, I will touch on some of the more popular modifications of desktop search today, but this idea of only investing where the user is will always be relevant. Investing in SEO that satisfies some arbitrary futuristic checkbox is not going to drive revenues and growth for a business, even if the effort drives increase in search engine visibility. The business category and type of customer are two of the biggest factors in how, or even if, you should invest in SEO. Visibility only matters when you are visible to the right user.

For many categories, especially long-sales-cycle B2B, SEO is absolutely the wrong investment. For others, it's the right one.

B2B VERSUS B2C SEO

The tactics and strategies for SEO are very similar whether the target customer is a consumer, business, non-profit, or government. In all cases, the goal is to maximize organic visibility to whoever is looking for a particular website or content. (Don't believe the naysayers; search is always part of the buying process. If you don't yet see how search will fit into your acquisition efforts, it's not because it doesn't exist; it's because you haven't yet found it.)

The goal of SEO is always the same—visibility. The means will vary.

The real difference in strategies between all the various end-user experiences is the expectations of how SEO will perform on that site and what kind of content should be optimized. Generally, the person conducting an organic search for a B2B product is much higher in the funnel than a user that comes in from an advertising channel.

For consumers, it is far more likely to have a conversion happen in the same session as the organic click. Business buyers generally take a little longer, and content should be crafted differently to reflect this fact. As we've talked about before, it's important to know the expectations of each type of user and the breakdown in the types of content that should be created for each use case.

All of these breakdown buckets will be fairly broad. Your consumer could be a teenager looking for an idea for an article for a high school paper or a high-net-worth individual seeking a financial advisor. Your business buyer could be a sole proprietor buying for their business or a buyer for a Fortune 500 company. The same SEO principles apply in all cases, but different approaches may be needed to serve each specific user.

With that in mind, here are the major buckets to consider:

- **Consumer**—Usually, the consumer is buying for themselves with few decision-makers; therefore, the buying process is quicker. The consumer wants the information they are seeking quickly. If they have purchase intent, they want to be reassured the purchase is worthwhile. Content for a consumer should be conversion-oriented.
- **Business**—At any medium or large company, there will be lots of decision-makers, so the goal of the content should be to get the search user to become aware of the brand. Content should be written to get the user to search more or share information with an email list or database. SEO efforts may have to aim a bit lower to have users join a webinar, for example, rather than buy products.
- **Non-profit**—A non-profit functions like a business in its buying behavior, except they are often more budget-conscious. Keep in mind a non-profit could be subsisting anywhere in the large range from a small local PTA to a global organization like the Red Cross. Don't make any assumptions.
- **Government**—Governments can range from local cities all the way up to national federal agencies. They often function like businesses with the clock rewound to a century ago. The content for government buyers has to establish the business as an entity worth exploring and should focus on building internal advocates. Understand individual governmental entities and their buying processes—and target those users.

Depending on the nature of the product, SEO might serve as

a very valuable awareness bucket. Attendees of trade shows or conference presentations might search the business name to find out more information. If the business has neglected SEO, there may never be hope for a follow-up conversation. Too often, B2B SEO campaigns fail because there was an expectation of instant conversions. Understand upfront, SEO's purpose is to assist. SEO, if done correctly, will set your business up for the jump shot—and the slam-dunk.

Knowing that SEO for B2B, government, or non-profit is there only to assist other channels in being more successful will go a long way in having SEO efforts that everyone is on board with supporting. This knowledge is also helpful in deciding if you should and, if so, how you focus on non-desktop search via mobile devices.

MOBILE SEO

With the rise of mobile in the collective marketing consciousness, there are some who think they need a separate mobile SEO strategy. For most sites, this approach would be entirely unnecessary and might even force them to split their resources unnecessarily. At its core, any mobile-marketing strategy is just a traditional web-marketing effort made for a smaller screen.

Google ranks websites on mobile optimization the same way it does on a desktop. The nuances between SEO for desktop and mobile are in how users interact with search and websites after they click.

From a search perspective, websites that rank highly for a query on desktop are going to rank equally on a mobile screen; however, there are fewer results, meaning a number-five slot on mobile is essentially like being on page two of results.

MOBILE-FIRST INDEX

Google announced in 2019 that it is using a mobile-first index, which isn't as ominous as it sounds. A mobile-first index merely means Google is ranking the content of a website that is visible to a crawler that emulates a mobile browser.

Mobile-first means that if a website were to have content served only to desktop users, Google would likely never find it as it crawls and indexes the content visible to mobile users.

Google's motivation behind having a mobile-first index is that in a mobile-first world, webmasters should make every effort to make all their content—or at least their best content—visible to mobile browsers.

USER-EXPERIENCE OPTIMIZATION

Google recommends having a mobile-responsive site that will look and function great on a mobile, tablet, or desktop environment. Longer menus should be collapsed rather than hidden completely. Content should be paginated or scaled rather than removed.

Although it might take some effort to implement a responsive site, this recommended approach might end up costing significantly less than having mobile-only and desktop-only sites. Much worse is not having a great mobile experience.

If a significant number of users are going to be using mobile devices, the entirety of your layout and content has to be mobile-user friendly. Mobile optimization, or mobile-friendly, means buttons have to be readily visible and effortless to tap. Images should load quickly, and the page should scale to the size of the screen.

A mobile SEO strategy is really just optimizing content as anyone might do on a desktop-only site. For your site, ensure the technology serving the content is friendly to mobile users.

OPTIMIZING FOR USER EXPERIENCE IS A KEY PART OF ANY SEO STRATEGY

Optimization for user experience should be done for any user regardless of the device they use. In the very likely scenarios where there are more mobile users than desktop users, optimizing for smaller devices should take precedence.

In the same light, there are going to be sites that should not bother with any mobile optimization at all. If there are primarily desktop users on these sites—say, a service like a complex web utility or B2B tool—it may not be worth the effort and resources to optimize for mobile.

Keep in mind, if a website is starting from scratch, design for mobile should play a role. For an existing website, the tradeoffs to optimize for mobile may not be worth the expense.

I find it hard to believe there will be many sites that could completely ignore mobile for all products or services. However, if expenses and resources are a concern, it is worthwhile to calculate the ROI before making a substantial investment in mobile. As always, consider your product and users before making decisions. SEO decisions should be product-led.

While mobile was last decade's big paradigm shift in SEO, this decade is going to be all about voice and smart assistants.

VOICE SEARCH

Given all the attention voice search gets in the media, you wouldn't be alone in thinking traditional search is going to cease to exist in the very near future. To think traditional search might stop is a prospect of terrifying proportions for many who rely on organic or even paid search as a primary source of attracting online users and customers.

In my opinion, we will never see a day where search has completely moved to voice only, and there are a number of reasons why this is true.

FINANCIAL

First and foremost is the profit motive of Google and other search engines. If Google were to give only a single result in response to a voice query, and that result was organic, Google could no longer monetize queries. From a raw financial perspective, it is unlikely Google would ever give up any of its juggernaut of paid advertising.

In addition, Google has increasingly moved in the direction of more paid search options, not less. Over the last few years, Google has placed more of its search engine page layout in the hands of advertisers.

Throughout the history of search, and especially paid search, there have rarely been instances where there has been just one paid result for a query. Even if Google were to give a paid response (and it's unclear how that might work) for a voice query, that would have to be just one paid advertiser and not the multiples they do now. Google would essentially be making the top advertiser the only advertiser.

SEARCH OPTIONS

While there is a lot of pressure in the organic world to obtain a top ranking on a Google query, by no means do the lower-ranking results get zero clicks. There are even clicks that happen on search-result pages well beyond the first one. This is because search is far from perfect. Even though Google uses AI to read minds and understand what a user wants, many times, even the user doesn't know what they are looking for.

There need to be multiple results so users can find exactly what they are looking for. A world of only voice search takes away those multiple options.

REFINED SEARCHES

A user will search, click a result, go back, click another result, or even conduct another search in their quest to find the information they seek. The very diversity of multiple results is what helps the user determine the best result. This process cannot ever be reproduced purely by voice simply because giving a single result to a query would mean Google would have to know EXACTLY what the user wants. (Even for Google, this is impossible.)

Knowing exactly what the user will click is easier when there's only one possible result, like a query on weather, numbers, directions, or the names of sports players. But knowing what the user is trying to find gets much harder when the results are completely subjective, such as finding the best vacation spot, the latest play-by-play of a game, or an opinion piece on the news.

Even with full personalization, it is impossible to know exactly what a user wants unless the user explicitly says what they want.

The user saying precisely what they want, of course, happens at times, but usually, a specific question is the final query in a series.

Imagine this query train:

- Best hotel in Miami
- Best Marriott hotel in Miami
- Marriot hotel in Miami with free parking
- Marriott hotels with suites and free parking
- Marriott hotel with suites, free parking, has a lounge
- Address of Marriott Biscayne Bay Miami

What you might notice is all the queries in that chain have multiple answers, and it would be completely impossible for Google to give just one response to all except the last one.

In the future, we might see voice-search prompts after a query is done, but that might only be applicable in a place where a user can't do a full desktop or mobile search, like in a car. More than likely, this whole clarification process will take so long and be so cumbersome, users will prefer a visual search with multiple responses over a long conversation with a smart (but dumb) device.

Essentially, the number-one reason voice search is never going to replace multiple results is voice must be perfect, and perfect is never possible in our changing world. Perfect will always change as users realize how much information it is possible to obtain by just conducting an online search for information.

Ten years ago, who could have ever imagined people would be able to ask their phones to read them a recipe or tell them whether they need to bring an umbrella? In the future, we may be able to ask our devices if we have the flu based on a number of symptoms, but we are likely not going to be able to find the perfect gift idea for a special someone with one voiced search option. While every site should always think of how it might "appear" on voice search, the business category will dictate how much voice search might disrupt the current way of searching.

Like voice, another SEO arena that will have large implications for some and be a non-issue for others is international SEO.

INTERNATIONAL SEO

International SEO is a very broad bucket that ranges from a US-based website widening its audience to include English-speaking Canadians to a US-based English-only website translating their content into Spanish while still only targeting US visitors. Of course, anything cross-language for a different country falls under this umbrella.

The first time I was faced with an international SEO challenge, I remember being completely baffled. I had no idea where to start. I had plenty of SEO experience but absolutely no background in doing SEO in languages I did not understand. As I started to dig into the SEO potential of the sites I was working with, I discovered that given the existing lack of optimization to foreign markets, the largest area of potential growth was going to be international SEO.

I discovered only just over 10 percent of the global internet population speaks English. I also learned US internet users were just over 6 percent of the total web users in the world. By focusing only on English speakers in the US, the global product we were selling was missing out on the vast majority of total potential users.

I decided I had to learn how to do international SEO.

As a result, I dove in blind and came up with a process that allowed me to build global SEO campaigns, even for languages I did not understand.

As a first step: don't make assumptions. There are multiple examples of companies that have gotten themselves into some pretty big PR disasters by using faulty assumptions in their global expansion. For example, KFC famously launched in China with a marketing slogan that meant "Eat Your Fingers" in Chinese. In hindsight, it seems some very basic research would have informed KFC they were making a big mistake with their messaging.

Are you sure your product or service is wanted in other regions or languages? It's vital you do your homework before you decide on a game plan. A good starting place is to look at demographic data in your current analytics tool. If you are currently receiving visitors from places around the world, it is likely you already have unfulfilled demand for your product.

KEYWORDS

Choosing correct keywords is even more important in non-English search simply because Google's algorithm is not as robust for languages other than English, and you won't benefit from synonym matching and spelling correction at the same level you do in English.

It doesn't do you any good to just grab a primary keyword from

Google Translate or the Google Keyword Tool. If the suggested word isn't one a native speaker would naturally use, you will be unlikely to see the international search traffic you are expecting, and the users that do find the site won't think your content is very high quality.

Here's my process for international keyword research:

1. Use Google Translate or another tool to search all your primary keywords. Gather ALL of the translation possibilities into a spreadsheet. Be sure to search single words as well as phrases, as translations will change.
2. Put all your keywords from your spreadsheet into a keyword-volume tool, like Google's Keyword Tool, Ahrefs, SEMRush, Rank Ranger, or any tool that you currently use.
3. Take the highest volume keywords and manually search them in Google.
4. Take note of any and all sites that seem to be in your competitive set.
5. Add all these sites into another worksheet in your spreadsheet.
6. Now for the fun part: start perusing all your competitor sites.
   A. Use a two-tab approach in Chrome, with one tab being the site as it is written in its original language and the second tab translated by Google Translate.
   B. Start noting all the important words used in title tags, menus, and calls to action and add them to a third workbook in your spreadsheet.
   C. Do this for every site in the results set, INCLUDING WIKIPEDIA.
7. Now that you have a spreadsheet with lots of words, it's time to pick winners. Take the highest volume words us‸ '
   on competitor sites. These will become your targe† '

8. Implement the keywords on a staged version of your site.
9. Make sure you are using the exact spelling and accents you discovered from your research.
10. Hire a native speaker on Craigslist, Upwork, or Freelancer.com to proofread and give feedback.
11. Launch your site live into the world.
12. Begin tracking the rankings of these keywords in Google Search Console or any standard SEO-visibility tool.
13. Iterate as necessary!

CONSERVATIVE ASSUMPTIONS MAKE MARKETING BORING

I am sure any marketer is well aware that a US holiday such as Thanksgiving isn't going to make a lot of sense to a non-US audience and would avoid using it in marketing copy. As a result, you might also assume references to the day after Thanksgiving as Black Friday wouldn't make sense to someone outside the US. This would be an incorrect assumption. Black Friday has been successfully exported around the globe, and many countries outside the US have Black Friday sales.

Do your research and learn your target market.

DON'T STEREOTYPE

Along the same lines, you want to avoid stereotyping cultures and languages. There are no countries called LatAm, Europe, and APAC (Asia). These names might be convenient buckets for allocating marketing dollars, but by no means will the same marketing message work across an entire region. Aside from the differing languages, a user in the UK has very different characteristics from someone in Germany. There are significant differences between a user in Mexico and a user in Colombia, both in the kinds of keywords they use and in the types of messaging they will respond to.

APAC is the broadest of all these buckets. This region has the most diverse languages and cultures when compared to other global markets. Democratic English-speaking Malaysia (English is one of the country's official languages) is very different from its neighbor monarchy and Thai-speaking Thailand. Many of the countries within this market aren't even close geographically. Sydney is a twelve-hour flight from Beijing.

USE DATA WHEN IT'S AVAILABLE

As anyone who has been working in online marketing for a while knows, there isn't always data to prove or disprove how every decision should be made, and many times, it will make sense to implement and analyze after the fact. In this reality, assumptions have their place, but you should certainly try to validate assumptions first.

BASIC INTERNATIONAL SEO IS NOT THAT HARD

Expanding your SEO efforts globally does not have to be prohibitively expensive or technically difficult. For example, you can make small changes as simple as explaining your primary product offering in another language. Say your site sells books written in English about Blue Widgets. If your entire site content is in English, your only non-English search traffic will be from users who conduct a search in English. However, if you translate your marketing content into Spanish, you can now draw in users who conduct their searches in Spanish. These users will still have to buy a book in English, but they will, at least, know that the book exists if they want it.

With just a few pages written in another language, your site can take a significant step toward acquiring a global audience. If you really want to take your global SEO efforts further, there is a lot more to do, but just having new content is a great start.

There really are baby steps you can take toward international SEO without getting in over your head. You can have just a handful of your marketing pages translated into languages from countries where you are already seeing visitors to your site. There will be a bit of work that has to go into translating and optimizing for a new language, but you should see a significant return on your investment. Just remember: if you are going to try to internationalize your site and product, do your research and know your market.

Just like international SEO is obviously not a fit for every business offline and online, business-to-consumer (B2C), mobile, and even voice SEO efforts, are not universally required. As I have suggested throughout this book, the most essential part of SEO is knowing your customers and building SEO around them. If you have a global product, focusing on only one geographic location would be a clear disservice to the broader customer base. The same, of course, is applicable to device- and channel-specific strategies. Creating a light mobile website is not ideal when you have a desktop audience who craves a rich experience.

B2B, B2C, and every other target market have subtle differences. Just as the same strategy wouldn't work in an offline world across channels as diverse as billboards and print ads, it also will not work with an SEO effort. Every distinction within your market matters. Rather than ignore what could be a key advantage, embrace those distinctions. Identify your audience, know your buyer, and create for that persona. This knowledge becomes power and will lead directly to the most successful SEO plans possible.

Then it becomes a matter of rolling out your SEO plan throughout your company.

THE COMPANY AND SEO

I had the opportunity to consult with a fascinating company that I believed had a tremendous upside to capitalize on organic traffic. I had met the CEO at an external event, and it was on her recommendation that I had been hired by the CMO to help build a strategic SEO effort. With that level of executive buy-in, I assumed it would be smooth sailing to implement the plan I developed with the team. How wrong I was.

After spending a couple of months working with the CMO and the tactical SEO teams to build out an SEO strategy and implementation plan, we packaged it up to share with the Executive teams for their feedback. Our plans were quite ambitious and would require the support of the Technical and Product teams.

We hit a roadblock almost immediately when we learned the Chief Technology Officer (CTO) had not allocated any engineering time at all that calendar year toward SEO projects.

Even small requests would mean something already planned for would not get done. Even worse, the Chief Product Officer (CPO), who had been clamoring for an SEO solution for years, had since given up. There was now no room on the Product roadmap for any SEO work.

Without the support of the Engineering and Product teams, the plan and assets I had built with the Marketing team were left without a way to ever put them in motion. Of course, the CEO could have demanded the Engineering and Product teams make room for SEO, but that is not a good way to demonstrate leadership. Fortunately, the CMO and I were able to negotiate with the Engineering and Product leaders, and they were able to slot some of our requests alongside previously planned work.

Prior to this experience, I had always believed executive buy-in meant having a single executive that would be willing to push SEO initiatives, but it turns out this is not enough. Unless you are or are working with an authoritarian leader who controls all aspects of a company, SEO is going to need the support of leaders across the company.

Even if you are not in a leadership position but are an employee of a large company, this chapter is for you. Large companies have unique bureaucratic ticks not present in small companies, and without knowing how to navigate the bureaucracy gauntlet, even highly competent people find success remains out of reach.

This chapter will discuss some of the large-company challenges and strategies for overcoming them. As in many unhealthy situations, the first step is acknowledging the problem exists, and big companies act really differently than you might expect.

BIG-COMPANY SEO, SMALL-COMPANY SEO

In a small organization or on a simple website, best SEO practices are easy to follow and implement. The person implementing the best practices might even have access to the CMS or other backend tools to make changes on their own.

As an organization grows or a site becomes more complex, following SEO best practices means there will be tradeoffs in other parts of the company or on the website. For example, there may be an ideal way to set up URLs, but it may break an entire shopping-cart experience. There needs to be a prioritization exercise on whether the SEO best practice trumps other business needs. The tradeoff is what I typically term "enterprise SEO," but I prefer the more descriptive "SEO at scale."

The rules and guidelines for SEO at scale are the same for every site, regardless of whether the site has ten pages or a million pages. Every site and every page, regardless of size, needs to have optimized metadata, great content, and good backlinks that vouch for the site.

A site like WashingtonPost.com doesn't get a pass for thin content just because it has a great brand, nor does Amazon.com get away with weak metadata. However, executing SEO is different at scale.

WHAT IS SEO AT SCALE?

Following best practices, implementing sitewide changes, and getting organizational buy-in are easy in small companies or on simple websites. For this explanation, I'm defining a simple website as a website that has very clean architecture. Also, a simple website is limited in size and structure; it has a homepage with a few subpages that might have a few of their own subpages. A blog is a great example of a simple website: there is a homepage, and every subsequent page is organized by date with a few tags thrown in.

Quite the opposite is true at larger organizations and on complex websites. Making changes in these environments is akin to turning an aircraft carrier—far from simple. From a company-culture perspective, the keys to approving the change may require intense collaboration with different departments, and even small changes might require consensus across various stakeholders. In a large organization, something as simple as a title-tag update might require the approval of various Product and Engineering managers, and sometimes, it might even need a Legal team's approval.

Once a change is approved, the actual rollout is directed in a standard engineering queue designed to keep websites and products bug-free by forcing all code changes into a process-driven system. The entire process is slow.

The corporate system, by its very nature, precipitates many touchpoints that make SEO incredibly difficult. This cedes advantages on search to smaller, more nimble organizations. (Note: If you are competing on search with a large competitor, know that you have the advantage, as they can never adopt change as fast as a smaller company.)

LARGE-COMPANY PROCESS

Large companies have factors like dedicated sprints that hold back even small SEO changes from nearly ever being released on the fly. There could be multiple layers of QA requiring the approval and understanding of engineers to clear a change for release. However, for anyone working on SEO in a large organization, nothing is as frustrating as the dreaded prioritization roadmap.

Prioritization Roadmap

Any change, even a small one, that requires engineering time must beat out other engineering requests in order to make it into a quarterly planning roadmap. The determining factor on the change is whoever is codifying that roadmap must believe the SEO effort will be as impactful as *something else* the SEO might bump off the roadmap.

If the person making the SEO request can't articulate (clearly and with urgency) the importance of their ask, the request will never have a chance. The only chance of a change happening, in that case, would require an engineer having "extra" time, and no good engineer will intentionally allow that to happen—ever.

In this environment of constantly second-guessing, the key skill of an SEO expert cannot be just their creative and analytical abilities. The SEO specialist will also need to possess political and diplomatic savvy. The person leading SEO at scale needs to have even stronger SEO abilities than they would in a smaller company. They will need to articulate the what, why, and how in a setting that could be potentially hostile to SEO asks.

Your SEO leader will need to know when an SEO best practice is really a key requirement and when it's just a good-to-have. The leader will have to be deployed as a key player in the horse-trading, back-scratching, and negotiating that happens in any big company.

Data

Depending on the enterprise culture, the SEO leader may even need to be a data whiz who can participate in a data-driven conversation about what matters most to the organization. Further complicating all requirements of SEO, data might not even be readily available. Key data crucial to decision-making might be locked up due to security necessities and only accessible via a request process.

A strong SEO leader or specialist will know how to operate within the confines of the data they can readily access while still knowing how to effectively translate it into the reporting metrics that the organization requires.

Small companies may utilize only one system of record, such as Google Analytics, while larger companies will have multiple tools and databases that each serve a different purpose. Negotiating the system in a larger company is part of the essential skill set.

PEOPLE

On the people side, there are also some pretty big differences between big and small companies.

Smaller companies will have direct points of contact for specific requests, and when those contacts transition out of the organization, the contact data will be replaced by another single individual. The same cannot be said at larger organizations, where reorganizations might happen multiple times per year.

As individuals leave large corporations, their responsibilities may shift to a new department, multiple people, or a new person coming into a role that had not existed before. The owners and leaders of various department sections might be in different offices that could even be a flight apart. Building relationships in the case of change in proximity requires being a pro at virtual communication.

An SEO leader or specialist could take months selling an effort to an individual or team only to have that entity no longer be able to implement the requirements when the time comes. Again, an SEO professional with strong, soft skills will be able to thrive in this environment, as they know how to find the new right contact and build the new relationship with ease.

ADVANTAGES

On the flip side, there are some amazing advantages to being able to do SEO at scale. At a smaller organization, the SEO team may be capped in their career path unless they move to another functionality. An SEO specialist at a large company can continue to get promoted as their impact grows.

If SEO efforts grow in importance, the team focused on SEO will grow; over time, they might be able to move into leadership roles as the department expands. Most importantly, the ROI from a large company's SEO efforts could easily be in the billions of dollars, justifying every cent spent on SEO. At a smaller company, the economics may not be as obvious, especially for those who don't know where to look.

LEARNING

Larger organizations provide more opportunities for continuous learning, and the SEO professional might find they can explore new responsibilities without giving up their current ones. The most significant benefit to an SEO specialist at a large company is the ability to get information not available at smaller companies.

With a website that is relatively small, it will be nearly impossible to ever get statistical significance from an SEO test. Larger websites afford many opportunities for testing, experimentation, and proof. The complexity of a large website can consistently be the best teacher of all. Knowing best practices around site hierarchy pales in comparison to actually learning what works best on a million-page website.

On a smaller website, international SEO might be limited to translating a contact page, while on a larger website, the work might entail translating a full website into ten different languages.

International operations open up a whole new realm of testing and learning as the SEO team now needs to contend with keywords in languages they don't understand, competitors thriving in other cultures, and a new set of rules around search engine discovery. When it comes to content duplicated across languages or countries, the right SEO professional will find this challenge a great opportunity.

SEO AND SEARCH ENGINE PERSPECTIVE

From a search engine perspective, SEO is the same for every website, but the effort that it takes to get there will vary widely depending on the complexity of the website and company. While many might think brands get a leg up in search—and it's very probable they do—brand advantages will only happen when all other factors are even.

Given the hoops large companies have to jump through to produce the same result as a small company, any gain is far from guaranteed. Smaller companies may actually have the advantage in many contexts.

As anyone who has ever worked on SEO at scale knows, getting to the ideal state on all SEO factors is like climbing a mountain…at night…in a snowstorm…while you're half-frozen. You know the peak is somewhere up there, and you just need to keep trudging forward. While the peak might take a long time to scale, if you stay the course, you will get there.

Everyone else might be on to the next mountain already, but you will stand at the summit, feeling a heroic sense of accomplishment at completing something that took a monumental effort.

SUCCEEDING AT SEO INCREMENTALLY

The best way to be successful in a process-driven large company is to always keep the focus on small, incremental wins. Little wins will ladder up into bigger wins; the small wins will add up in the impact they have within a company. Building a detailed plan for incrementality is so much more effective than creating a plan that will never get executed unless there are executive buy-in and a dearth of initiatives across the company—which, of course, there never will be.

Proposing a complete website revamp is a surefire way to a back burner and the purgatory of no budget, but a refresh of a particular page is a far easier sell. The page refresh might need to be implemented piecemeal, but at least it's not a project size that makes stakeholders recoil in fear. Incremental progress is doable and successful.

SMALL WINS

When setting these small-win targets, it's really important to make the little wins as small as possible. Just changing the title of a page could be surprisingly difficult at a large company. Even getting buy-in from a cross-functional counterpart may be a meaningful marker if it's not a given when each team or department has very individualized goals.

Within small companies with only a handful of employees, culture can be set by founders, and a company can be oriented toward results. As an organization grows, processes are introduced that can add levels of complexity to getting things done. Much of these processes will be vital for the future success of the company, but inevitably, they will also lead to bureaucracy. For a growth-minded Product manager or marketer, the bureaucracy can be negated by embracing incremental wins as a method to succeed.

While it is easier to "get things done" in a smaller company, you shouldn't just throw up your hands at a large company and give up. Initiatives absolutely do get executed at bigger companies; it's just that the pathway to making things happen is a bit windy, and there are a lot more rest breaks along the way.

Work with the processes and structure you have.

SEO IS A PRODUCT FUNCTION

One of the reasons a company may leave its SEO potential unfulfilled is because it inadvertently silos in the person or people responsible for SEO. The company leaves the responsible SEO party on their own as an individual contributor, forced to go through their manager to get anything done.

This organizational structure is because SEO is often viewed as a Marketing function. Tasks are structured as campaigns relying on other Marketing contributions, such as Content and Design. Technical tasks like building or launching a page happen somewhere else in another divisional org structure within the company.

Instead, SEO should be viewed as a Product in and of itself. In this way, the engineering tasks would be a part of the Product roadmap and launch process from the start. Product managers are akin to a symphony conductor, and their roles are always reliant on other teams and inherently cross-functional.

Having SEO functioning as a Product does not necessarily need to change its reporting structure. In many cases, it makes perfect sense for SEO to be on the Marketing team. Approaching SEO as a Product function helps clarify its inputs and outcomes on multiple levels.

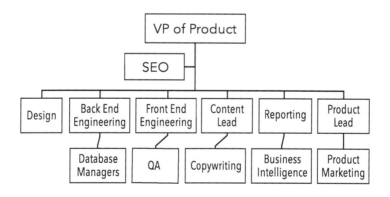

PLANNING

When planning for SEO goals, it is critical all required resources from other teams be allocated at the exact same time.

It wouldn't make a whole lot of sense to plan to launch a collection of pages or a new micro-site and not pre-allocate the Design time and Engineering plan.

On the Product-Management side, new initiatives are never approved with a hope and a prayer that everything will just work out when the time is right. All products that are prioritized will get the resources to complete the project. Shifting SEO to a Product function means it deserves and will receive planning and resources on time.

BUDGETING

When it comes to budgeting on a Marketing plan, SEO usually falls to the bottom of the pile since the story on investment to output is harder to sell to the Chief Financial Officer (CFO). Traditionally, this means SEO will get the short end of the stick for the hiring of software and contractors, whereas Paid-Marketing teams might be flush with cash.

Thinking instead of SEO as a product realigns the expectations on investment. A product—by its very nature—needs investment because it is a priority, even if it is one on a long-time scale. Typically, Product teams aren't resourced because they have a direct line to ROI but, rather, because the product is a business necessity.

OUTPUT AND REPORTING

On the same note, when SEO is thought of as Marketing, it needs to be measured similarly to other Marketing KPIs. Paid-Marketing teams have customer lifetime value (LTV) goals (hopefully), and Brand teams have their impression share, leaving SEO to be measured on rankings alone.

Having SEO relegated to mere rankings is a terrible way of measuring progress. As we've discussed, rankings are just a vanity metric. Instead, we should measure SEO the same way any product is measured: by adoption and engagement. A good metric is growth in impressions on search pages. Obviously, clicks are important too, but the clicks are a result of on-page structure, which is not necessarily SEO itself.

RESOURCING

Making the case to add more headcount for SEO can be very difficult if the metrics for success are too hard to reach or inappropriate for the channel. When we view SEO as a product, the primary headcount metric moves from being KPI-driven to deadline-driven. The question that should be asked is, "What is the headcount necessary to meet the goal within the desired timeframe?"

Not much really has to change on reporting, salary, and even titles to make SEO more aligned with Product. When SEO is aligned with Product, it mostly changes awareness and Management.

If the current method for managing SEO is leaving value on the table, it may be helpful to change the structure of how SEO should be conducted within a company. An investment in SEO is an investment in a growth channel. If SEO is incorrectly viewed as a hygiene item, part of a Marketing checklist, understandably, there may not be excitement about giving resources to it. Viewing it through the prism of growth, however, the ROI calculation is far easier to develop. Those things that matter, however, should also be planned for.

PROJECT MANAGEMENT FOR SEO

Managing SEO as a Product means SEO asks will have to fit within a typical project-management or Product-prioritization process. In many organizations, Product requests must be accompanied with detailed information that would allow a Product manager to stack rank any request against any other priority. The paperwork should include details that would help managers calculate the resources and time needed to complete the request.

Remember that stack ranking was popularized forty years ago, in the 80s, and should maybe be retired for certain purposes, for example, in the case of SEO.

While every organization will have its own format, here's a format for SEO requests I have found to be incredibly useful.

	Fix Title Tags	**Build a Site Map**
Why is this a problem?	Title tags are essential for SEO	Many pages on the site are not indexed and a sitemap will help crawlers find all pages
Recommended fix	Add keywords to all title tags	Create an XML sitemap of all published pages
Impact (1–10)	10	5
Effort (high score= low effort)	5	5
Confidence (score 1–10)	10	5
Priority (sum of prior rows)	25	15
Notes	We can use an intern to do this	We should crawl the whole site first and create folders based on taxonomy
Jira ticket	jira-12345	jira-12346
Assigned date	12/1/19	12/1/19
Assigned to	Bob	Lisa
Completed date		
Completion notes		
Other notes		

COLUMNS EXPLANATION

1. The first column has a quick summary of the ask.
2. The second column goes into a bit more detail on why the thing needs to be fixed. This should be explanatory enough that someone could understand it just by reading the spreadsheet.
3. Column three should explain the fix as well as any alternative options. The options will give the Product manager all

the information they need to go about assigning the request to any stakeholder.

4. Column four scores the impact of the fix on a scale of one through ten, with ten being the most impactful.
5. Column five scores the effort related to making the fix on a scale of one through ten, with ten being the lowest effort. A ten might be a quick text fix, while a one could be a full rebuild.
6. As with anything SEO-related, there is a certain amount of guesswork that goes into planning, so in the sixth column, I score the confidence of the impact and effort on a scale of one through ten.
7. Column seven calculates the stack ranking by adding up the scores. A higher score is the most impactful, lowest effort, and highest confidence of success.
8. The next few columns are for tracking and coordination. Column eight has additional notes not captured previously.
9. Column nine records a bug ticket, so anyone looking to follow along on progress knows where to look.
10. Column ten has the date it shipped to Engineering, which is very helpful for bunching work into quarters.
11. In column eleven, we see the assigned person, so anyone checking on the progress knows whom to talk to.
12. The rest of the columns have additional notes that are very helpful for future tracking.
    A. Completed dates
    B. Notes

Too often, SEO requests are ignored or not assigned because there is not enough clarity on what is being requested.

Using a detailed spreadsheet like this (or whatever process is comfortable for company culture) will ensure SEO asks follow the same model as any other product that comes in front of the Engineering, Marketing, or Product teams.

Having a detailed spreadsheet, such as this one, is also very helpful to have handy when there's a sudden need to share progress with an executive. The spreadsheet will preserve and display a clear list of what has been accomplished or where things are in the pipeline. Additionally, this document is great to hand over to other employees when the SEO person moves on from the company.

QUARTERLY AND ANNUAL SEO PLANNING

In addition to shorter days and colder nights (at least in the Northern Hemisphere of the world), September brings a special gift to the office that everyone claims to welcome. But in truth, they all despise it. We are, of course, talking about annual planning.

Many large companies will have some sort of quarterly planning process where teams will have to detail how they have progressed on the current quarter's goals. The progress check-in must also detail what the team member hopes to accomplish in the coming quarter.

ANNUAL PLANNING

While this process isn't necessarily the most fun, it can be straightforward. There isn't much artistry or charm in the annual planning process, which is typically conducted in the closing quarter of a year and requires a team to pick a goal for the coming year. Negotiating for the resources to achieve said goal can be off-putting and strangling for teams that are often denied the essentials.

However, there is great benefit in making predictions about things, issues, and plans that are already in flight. Getting resources to fund goals is also critical.

WINNING AT ANNUAL PLANNING

Teams that "win" the annual planning process, in the sense that their goals are accepted and their resource requests are met, can, in many ways, rest for the next twelve months until the process begins again.

In most organizations, a team will not necessarily be held to their goals because, of course, a lot can change over a year. A team's real win is that they were given the resources (defined as budget and headcount) to meet their goals. If they did not meet that goal for whatever external reason, they are still able to deploy the resources to make some other flashy business impact.

This business impact—even if it was not the one stated in the annual planning process—positions them in a very good light the following year. Next year, just like last year, the team states lofty goals and requests resources to help them get to those lofty goals.

LOSING AT ANNUAL PLANNING

On the flip side of the teams that win the planning process are the teams that "lose." These are the teams whose goals are not adopted as goals worthy of being resourced, and their requests will be turned down in favor of other teams.

These disenfranchised teams will still have a required goal for the coming year. They will likely need to water-down that goal due to the lack of resources. These teams could likely find themselves generally deprioritized and locked out of new headcount and budget wins for an entire year.

When it comes time to develop goals and make requests for resources in the following year, these teams also start off with a significantly weaker hand. Being minimized, they also don't have the benefit of having made a huge impact in the prior year.

Looking at planning in this light, the stakes could not be higher. Teams must win at the planning process and successfully pitch executives. Lacking support (and an executive) behind goals, teams will be at risk of becoming nonessential line items until something fundamentally changes in the business.

The only exception to this rule is if there is a high-level executive backing a team or if there is a shift in power within a company. Shifts in power come in the forms of a reorganization, fundraising event, or new Product need.

Due to the nature of where SEO teams often sit within a large organization, they regularly begin this planning process behind the curve. In most companies, SEO either sits within Marketing or Product, and this placement has a big effect on how they do in a planning process.

SEO IN MARKETING

If an SEO team is a part of the Marketing team, they likely report to a Marketing leader of some sort. The Marketing leader will be juggling budget and headcount requests from teams that can make far stronger 1+2 = 3 pitches. For example, a Paid-Marketing team can show very clear math of how an additional paid budget will impact acquisition, retention, or awareness. Marketing can also show how an added headcount will improve the efficiency of its spend, thereby adding more value to the organization.

The same argument might work for a Content team that could show how output (the metric that Content teams are measured by) will improve by a factor of how much more is spent on producing content.

Contrast that with the SEO team that has fuzzy math for how SEO works and even fuzzier math for what more spend might produce. The SEO pitch for resources is a losing proposition with Marketing teams' limited understanding of the nature of SEO. These reasons are why most SEO teams, even in companies with large Marketing sub-teams, will still only consist of one or two people.

SEO IN PRODUCT

When an SEO team sits on a Product team, the uphill climb to win resources is slightly easier but not by much. Rather than a pitch for just budget and headcount, the resource ask will also likely include engineering time.

In a company that does not prioritize SEO, the engineering time request might get shunted aside in favor of building new products or improving existing products or services.

Logically, tossing resources aside makes a lot of sense to heads of companies. What Product leader would rather have a roadmap full of improvements to existing products rather than a new shiny product or service with all sorts of exciting new builds? And yet, good SEO practices will pay off over the long term many times over.

HOW TO WIN RESOURCES

To win at the annual planning game, the SEO team must morph into the kind of team everyone loves to fund and support. The rule of "lovable" applies regardless of where the SEO team sits in the organization.

WHAT TO DISCARD TO WIN

First and foremost, the whole idea of using wishy-washy data to forecast SEO impact must be completely discarded. There is data within the company and Google Search Console that very clearly tells the story of how valuable SEO traffic is for top-line acquisition.

There will be data on how your SEO impacts the bottom line, too. Get that data and use it as the guiding light within an annual goal. Data doesn't lie and can't be argued against. Data provides proof.

Is the plan to increase SEO traffic by 10 percent? That's not a compelling goal! Revisit what a 10 percent organic traffic increase might mean to top-line revenue. Find the top and use that number as the goal. An increase of 10 percent of overall web revenue from organic sources sounds a whole hell of a lot sexier than an unclear 10 percent increase of traffic.

THE PITCH FOR THE WIN

Many other teams will pitch ideas they don't really know how they will implement but want resources to try. The other teams certainly aren't pitching the process on how they may or may not get there; rather, they are saying they are going to build X—and X requires engineers.

The SEO team should do the exact same thing.

Instead of asking the engineers to update a whole bunch of SEO requirements, ask for engineers (or content or money) to build X for SEO.

Third, and this is specific to each company, there is a process for how every other Product and Marketing team pitches for resources. Make sure the SEO pitch looks exactly the same and follows the course for resources already laid out in the company. There is data to show even greater impact from SEO than other efforts, if you assemble it.

Keep SEO jargon out of the pitch and use the same language that everyone else uses. The last thing an SEO team wants is to have their pitch stand out because no one understands what was talked about.

ANNUAL PLANNING FROM A LEADERSHIP STANDPOINT

The prior advice mostly applies to SEO practitioners pitching for resources or those pitching SEO asks to the C-suite, but it can just as well be modified for leaders being asked for the resources.

Know that SEO is incredibly important. If the pitch for resources doesn't have the clear 1+2 = 3 approach, push it back to the team for a revision. Don't reject the ask out of hand.

Annual planning is a process no one really enjoys, other than the people who run the process for everyone else. Annual planning will likely remain a necessary evil, and the procedure isn't going to go away if it is ignored.

If an SEO team does not put its best foot forward, it could risk losing an entire year of resources (funds, engineering, content) with a gain of zero impact efforts. Spend the time to do planning well.

Within a big company, SEO can be won or lost without even changing a line of code. Success can be just as much about how you advocate for the cause of SEO during annual planning as the actual technical or content plans you develop. Knowing how to play this game of strategy can be the difference between having an entire year where nothing of meaning changes or a year where a company pivots to the cause of SEO.

Rather than hide in the opaque space in which SEO typically operates, bring it out in the open and advocate for resources the same way every other team does. Use the same terminology, planning processes, and—most importantly—the KPI metrics of the entire company, and you will find you have the greatest chances of putting your SEO skills to use.

Some of the greatest SEO success stories on the internet didn't win because of domination in key SEO metrics. They won in how they were victorious in integrating SEO within the product and company, while their competitors were not. Think Amazon versus Walmart.com; NerdWallet versus the very banks and credit cards it reviews; or, even more specifically, Yelp versus all the restaurants on its platform.

In addition to embedding SEO within the culture of the company, these organizations are also models in Product-Led SEO and building for the user rather than for search engines.

CHAPTER NINE

IMPLEMENTING PRODUCT-LED SEO

I have had the opportunity to work with multiple phenomenal multi-disciplinary Product-Led SEO teams. Each team has worked together to implement SEO effectively as a product, and it has been a privilege to work with each of them.

However, one team stands out in my mind. This team was highly diverse in specialty; we had a senior executive, a Content manager, a project manager, a lead growth engineer, a data scientist, and myself as the SEO Product manager. The team, over time, began to function like a harmonious symphony. Each person had their own unique instrument and specialty that combined with the work of other team members to create beautiful music. The result was a stronger SEO product than any of us could possibly have created on our own, with lead generation and revenue to match.

Each person brought a unique contribution to the table and was fully empowered in their functional area. The executive had the clout to marshal resources, allocate budget, and sell the rest of the Executive team on strategy. The engineer did not have to rely on others to make decisions; he could make commitments to deliver on the spot according to his judgment. The Content lead fully controlled the Content roadmap. The project manager could reallocate resources anytime toward the broader SEO strategy. The Data Science lead could pull SEO-relevant data or initiate research at any time. Finally, I, as the Product manager, could make meaningful Product changes and recommendations without delays because everything I needed was right on the team I was on.

This team structure is the ideal one and not only possible at smaller companies; I have seen it happen in larger companies when there is massive SEO buy-in. However, having an executive participate in the SEO efforts on a daily basis is both the most difficult to get *and* the most valuable. When there is this level of buy-in, the team can be highly effective and will therefore continue to justify their own existence. The challenge is getting this level of buy-in to begin with. In the case of this standout team, I can't take the credit. Executive leadership had had prior experience with SEO, and they were sold on the idea of creating a dedicated team before I was ever involved.

However, you may not be this fortunate. Do not despair. The road will be longer but just as valuable. You may have to work within the confines and political structure that exist already, but as you become more successful at scaling SEO within your organization, you will earn political capital you can spend to make requests and even realign teams toward SEO needs. Everyone will want to jump on board a winning team and strategy. If you are in the fortunate minority that you have an SEO team ready to execute on the search opportunities in front of you, go ahead and grab it. For everyone else, likely in the majority, you will need to run Product-Led SEO strategically and carefully to unlock your full SEO opportunities.

SEO IS A MULTIDISCIPLINARY EFFORT

SEO impacts every aspect of an organization's sales cycle, from total brand visibility and top-of-funnel long-tail search to bottom-of-funnel immediate conversions. Every team, no matter its function, will impact or be impacted by the leads nurtured by SEO. As a result of its general impact, it's important to have SEO awareness and collaboration throughout the entire company. This is not a radical or surprising argument. What is surprising is how much the internal teams can be impacted positively by SEO efforts. The discipline is truly multi-disciplinary in both its requirements and impact.

In both my consulting and full-time roles, I have had meetings with teams that you would never have thought would need SEO input or output. I have met with Finance to discuss modeling SEO traffic for predicting revenue estimates to share with Wall Street. I've met with an HR department with a keen interest in ensuring that open job positions were highly visible in search. I've mediated disputes between Design and Engineering, prodding Design to make sure they didn't stretch the limits of what Engineering was able to do within the bounds of search friendliness.

My favorite cross-functional collaboration was when I worked with a Vice President of customer support to correct an SEO disaster on an externally-hosted support site. A mistake had been made that dramatically reduced the visibility of customer-support content that allowed customers to help themselves with solutions. Unable to find answers to their queries, confused customers resorted to calling and emailing the support team. This SEO issue had a very real cost in customer-support hours needed to answer all these questions.

SEO requires and impacts disciplines from across traditional siloes and, as such, is best run with a team pulled from a variety of disciplines.

PRODUCT TEAMS, NOT MARKETING

In many organizations today, the structure best suited to multi-disciplinary teams has been the Product structure. I believe SEO teams should sit within a Product organization rather than on a Marketing team. Marketing teams tend to approach efforts from a linear standpoint, and SEO might come all the way at the beginning or just at the end. Neither of these placements, at the extremes, is beneficial.

On the other hand, Product managers stay intimately involved with whatever they are working on, from ideation all the way through iteration post-implementation. If there is an existing Product team structure, I recommend rolling SEO efforts into this structure. Regardless, even if there is not, or if SEO is necessarily on a Marketing team, approaching SEO efforts from this lens will give the best results. SEO leaders should act like Product managers and insert themselves as a hub between many spokes, all providing unique input to the SEO product they are working on.

There may be some organizational friction around changing the process of how things are completed, but this will be far easier than insisting on moving teams and employees around, especially in a huge company.

To the degree it's possible to have each member of the team have the latitude to make decisions affecting their specialty, this is recommended. With autonomy to fully own their contributions, they are best positioned to collaborate with other functional leaders in building the best SEO effort possible, just like that ideal team I was a part of.

A NOTE ON HIRING THE PRODUCT MANAGER SEO ROLE

We've talked about the importance of finding the right people for SEO role(s) in an earlier chapter, but I'll make a quick additional note here. If you are running your SEO function as a Product function, as I recommend, you'll need a leader with the right skill set who is also able to function as a Product manager. (In very large companies, you may need several people in this kind of role with a single leader over all of them, but most companies can function with a single Product manager role.)

Ideally, you are the Product manager for the SEO product that is being created. However, if it is not you, this person could very well be the most important individual in the whole Product-Led SEO effort. They will champion the product to anyone who will listen, fight for resources, keep it in the minds of executives, and drive everyone to stay on deadline.

If you can't be this person, you will need to find a Rockstar that will be your counterpart and help drive massive success for SEO and the whole company. The Product manager leading the effort does not need to be an SEO expert if they have an internal or external expert working with them, but they do need to be amazing at wrangling people and whacking challenges. In order for this person to be as motivated as you, they will need to be brought into the vision. Show them the dream of what could come from successful SEO, work with them on the plan, and help them as much as possible to help you.

If this person is not you, interview with care. Focus on someone who can break the mold and drive progress rather than a person who just checks SEO boxes. The more cross-functional knowledge they have, the greater their effectiveness. (They should meet as many cross-functional internal partners as possible during the interview process to test them and their fit with the entire cross-functional ecosystem.) Even if they don't come in with coding abilities, a willingness to learn, SEO-based knowledge, and a comfort level with working with several disciplines will make them a huge asset.

Many of the people who have helped me the most in building out successful SEO strategies have been Product managers, and I am grateful to all of them for how they laid it all on the line to see things completed.

BUILDING THE SEO PRODUCT TEAM

Since you are building something that does not yet exist as a part of your Product-Led SEO approach, you will need the entire gamut of what a new product requires: Design for layout and structure, User-Experience (if separate from Design) to advocate for the optimal experience, content marketers and copywriters to write the text for the pages, Data Science and Analytics to build dashboards and reporting, and Engineering to build whatever it is that you are creating.

I've made some quick notes on what to look for in these functions in an SEO Product team specifically since each can function somewhat differently from a traditional Product role.

If you are jury-rigging cross-functional capability into a role that isn't a Product team, you may still wish to approach collaboration with these kinds of roles in a similar way. The more collaborative inputs you are able to seek out and address effectively, the stronger your final product is likely to be.

DESIGN

When it comes to building SEO products, Design is often neglected. Perhaps it seems far removed from the content that actually drives the SEO growth. However, since you are building a new product, it should get the same treatment as anything else that users engage with. Don't view designers as a stop on the road to a completed product; instead, partner with them and allow them to contribute their vision for the product's look and flow.

If you don't include Design in the early ideation part of your efforts, you might build something, start generating traffic, and only then go to designers for help. At this point, you'll require a complete rebuild from a design and user standpoint, and it will be far more work-intensive than the paint job you'll have at the beginning. This makes things infinitely harder to scale into a real product than if you had just included Design from the beginning.

USER/PRODUCT EXPERIENCE

In some organizations, there are separate teams that focus on user experience. If your company has a team like this, again, bring them in early, just like designers. Their input can easily make the difference between a very successful product or a mediocre one that does not resonate with the user base.

Additionally, User-Experience teams are more likely to help create a product when they are brought into the vision from the outset rather than if you offhandedly include them when the product is already a going concern. If you want to attract users, include User-Experience Design!

SUPPORT

Since you are building an actual product that provides something of use for users, expect there to be issues with how the product works—bugs and complaints. Someone needs to be there to address these real issues with users. Generally, I have found that Support teams are great resources for understanding customers and where pain points might come up as users navigate a product. Ultimately, when the product is live, you will need Customer Support to help manage it. However, you can also get a far better product by including them early on. Never ever underestimate how much your Support team knows about your customers.

In addition, there are significant gains from including them early in terms of their buy-in later. After the product is launched, most of the heavy lifting will fall on the Support team while you get to coast on the winnings. If you involve the Support team early on, they will often show up for you and the product they helped create in a much more powerful way later.

CONTENT

With Product-Led SEO, Content is incredibly important in the SEO process, but it is just one piece of the whole puzzle. In conventional SEO efforts, Content drives the train, and the whole effort will succeed or fail via the content that is created. Don't misunderstand, SEO will still fail with poor content in Product-Led SEO, but every other input that makes up the product is equally important.

Stay strong, and reject out-of-hand any attempt to promote keyword-driven content as the pathway to growth. (Content specialists, especially, may push this approach.) Don't entertain and don't recommend this strategy. In whatever seat you are sitting, always strive to understand the outcome of the effort. If the math behind keyword-driven content seems to be too fuzzy, it probably is. Don't double down on what you know to be ineffectual.

In Product-Led SEO, the metric for high-quality content is different than traditional SEO. Content is possibly programmatic and short form, rather than long form and keyword targeted. Rather than finding the best writer for the lowest price, you will instead seek out the best data sets to be turned into content by the most creative content writer. The investment in content will be more likely driven by purchasing data sets than the typical per-word cost for content marketing.

Even if content will be written programmatically, the content still has to be logical and useful for users. There's no value in hooking a user to click onto your result from a search engine page but then confuse them when they land on the page. If the content doesn't make sense, they are unlikely to act upon a call to action, and certainly, they will not give their credit card number.

The content in Product-Led SEO is a key part of the product, and it should be a key part of how the users engage with the product you have built for SEO. However, if you've done your thinking on the product correctly, you have more flexibility under this system. Unlike other parts of the product, content will be the most modular part, and if it is not working, you can change it. Additionally, as more information is learned, you can add more to the product and improve the user experience later.

Speaking of learning more information, you should have a way of knowing what in your efforts is working and what is not.

DATA SCIENCE

Data-Science teams are an embellishment over traditional Business-Intelligence teams responsible for reporting business metrics. Data scientists take the concept of reporting business outcomes and overlay it with complex modeling that could never be uncovered with standard analytics packages alone.

If you don't have access to a Data-Science team, don't give up and fly blind. Use the data you have and not the data you think you should have. Then, find a way to test and trial until you build the data you need. It is better to invest less because you don't have the best picture of what success looks like in a complex market than to invest too much when your assumptions are incorrect. Data science could help you prove that users who come into your SEO product spend more, but don't make up a hypothesis like this without actual data. Test and adjust.

Another advantage to data science in Product-Led SEO is that you can create richer parts of your SEO product as the Data-Science team could help you uncover data points not plainly available in existing data. If you were focused on specific cities as part of your product, as an example, you might be able to say how many active users are in each city, but only a Data-Science team could help calculate how many logins there are by each city or how much time each city spends using the product.

Having access to this data makes for a richer product page than anyone else could make. Product-Led SEO has the goal to build a product offering for search users that is unique and useful, and data science can actively help give that effort a leg up over competitors with similar web products. A powerful product with well-written content built on a well-engineered platform with exclusive data makes for a formidable go-to-market strategy.

ENGINEERING

If there was anywhere you don't want to cut any corners at all, it is in Engineering and Development. Someone has to build the product! Unlike the other teams you will work with, Engineering teams will have very different goals. It is your job to bring them into your vision. The Engineering team could achieve its goal of bug-free effective code in many ways, while there might only be one good way to achieve your goal of having a maximum-visibility SEO product. In other words, a fantastic product idea with great product-market fit is still doomed to fail if it is not built on the right platform.

Engineering and software development might not be something that you understand easily, but I would urge you to learn as much about them as possible. The more you know, the more likely you will be able to make effective requests of the Engineering team and earn their respect by knowing when to declare something a requirement versus a nice-to-have.

Don't be fooled, however. Technical engineering knowledge is not enough and, in fact, is easier to acquire than good people skills. Much of effective SEO Product management, especially in a large company, is about diplomacy, and nowhere else do you need more solid diplomatic skills than when working with engineers. Many times, you will be speaking a completely different language than them, yet you will want them to come along to your way of thinking just because you asked. Earning that level of political capital with engineers at all levels is no easy feat, and it will take effort. Invest in building these relationships. You will be glad you did when you come to an impasse, and your only currency is friendship.

EXECUTIVE

Remember the executive we had as part of our active team when I talked about the team at the beginning of this chapter? An executive is by far the hardest member to get and the most effective at accelerating progress by creating buy-in and delivering resources.

Now that you know what disciplines you'll need on your team, or at least will need input from, how do you get executive buy-in, whether or not they are involved in the day-to-day? How do you make the case?

MAKING THE CASE TO EXECUTIVES

However you decide to invest in SEO, whether via an external party or internally, you are going to need to get a lot of people on board. Depending on the culture and size of the company, this could be as simple as announcing it is a new initiative all the way to battling other teams in a cage match to get development time on a roadmap. Regardless of how hard or easy this is, your message should be the same: SEO is an important initiative with a significant amount of upside potential.

If you don't know the upside potential yet, don't pitch it until you do, and pitch it in the same KPIs as the rest of the business. Individuals pitching SEO don't do themselves any favors by specifically declaring there can be no apples-to-apples comparison or easy way to measure this channel. Doing anything different requires extra effort for the person you are attempting to convince. When you use the same KPIs, it is simpler for them to evaluate options and to say "yes."

If you already have SEO performance data from previous efforts, build the case for new investment into your SEO product from that data. From that, you should have a good sense of how an organic-search user will interact with your site and what their specific needs might be. You can then use that data to extrapolate into the expected growth of the channel.

Forecasting channel growth is where things become a bit more challenging. First and foremost, using keywords as a predictor of how much search traffic you can expect to generate is not a viable option for a few reasons. If you identify keywords that have high search volume, more than likely, there are search competitors that already dominate high-ranking positions for those queries. Assuming you will displace them is not realistic. Additionally, as you are focused on building a product toward a Blue Ocean based on customer research, there shouldn't already be keyword research to rely on as you build your model.

Without the ability to rely on keyword search as a north star for your new product, you need to find a proxy instead. Use a tangential product that might have similar demand, and use the search volume for that site. As an example, if you are creating a new database for healthcare pricing, you could use the total search traffic for sites that have offerings tangentially related to what you will offer. CMS.gov, HHS.gov, and healthcare.gov are all options. Use the total search-traffic numbers they get (finding those numbers with a tool like Ahrefs, SEMRush, or SimilarWeb) and then divide that by the number of content pages they have.

This quick calculation will give you an average estimate of monthly traffic per page that you can then use as input for predicting your own traffic. For starters, you can assume you will get at least this amount of traffic. You can also multiply this average traffic per page by the number of pages you will have, or if you are more conservative, multiply it by a percentage of the average. Finally, attach this number to an average visit value in dollars, downloads, or leads to get your business-goal number.

While this way of getting to a goal might seem somewhat finger in the air, it is far more reality-based than most SEO forecasts that use an unattainable keyword as the starting point, factor in a guessed clickthrough rate, arrive at a visit number, and then multiply that number by some other number. The result of my formula won't be an accurate estimation of traffic either, but you need a number you are targeting, and I find this approach to give more realistic and reasonable answers than conventional methods.

If you don't like this method of estimation, that's fine. You don't need a specific number. As you develop the proposal to build your SEO efforts, however, try to be as detailed as possible. Even if there are fuzzy numbers, come into these conversations with calculations just as anyone else asking for resources would. Build out the model in a way that reaches the same goals that everyone else in the company uses.

Whether you use hard numbers or not, however, any figure you do provide should certainly be bigger than the cost side of the equation, or no one will listen to your pitch.

Fortunately, outcomes are often better than you may assume on a short-term schedule. As you calculate potential returns, remember that you can use up to five years of payback time. In most marketing initiatives (brand excepted), payback only happens while the campaign is alive and the work is in progress. However, with SEO, there is a large upfront investment, with the payback coming in over time. In fact, long payback is realistic and common; I have had many initiatives continue to drive measurable returns for years.

The flip side to the long payback period is it could take an exceedingly long time before you see any results. As you make the pitch, be upfront and transparent about both of these points. The more transparency you have, the less likely you are to be surprised by the budget being pulled out from under you because there have been no meaningful returns on an executive's mental schedule.

In your proposal, ensure you have accurately made the ask for everything up front. In a small company, missing a resource could mean needing a new hire (which you may or may not get), while at a larger organization, not making the resource request could mean you will never be able to complete your project.

HAVE FAITH IN GOOD SEO PRODUCT STRATEGY

If you have done your research effectively in building out your Product plan and you execute as best as you can, expect that you will blow your forecast out of the water. (This is a common and realistic occurrence.) Your research indicated there was demand for your product, and all the search traffic will flow to you once your product exists. Most importantly, you will be creating the flywheel where demand begets future demand, as users tell other users about your product. These users will also search for your product offering on search engines, and the search engines will see there is demand for your offering since your website addresses a need that had previously been unmet.

In a nutshell, creating such a demand is the essence of the Product-Led SEO approach. It drives search engines as well as human users to gravitate toward your product offering and ultimately into whatever your core value proposition was before you even thought to build an SEO channel. Why play in someone else's market when you can create your own Blue Ocean?

STAY FLEXIBLE

An ancient Greek philosopher once said, "Change is the only constant in life," and this is an entirely appropriate way to sum up the practice and future of SEO.

Don't get too comfortable. You can be certain user behaviors will change over time. Therefore, without periodic updating, technical SEO efforts will quickly spiral into irrelevance. However, if we can embrace a solid strategy, we can stay flexible on the tactics. We can adjust the technicals over time to stay aligned like a gyroscope no matter where the demands of users and the progress of search technology take us. From this perspective, change is positive if it allows us to pull ahead of less-thoughtful competitors. SEO is the last bastion where a small business could be on the same footing as a major brand with deep pockets, and SEO can be a major driver of lasting business success.

The future is bright. User appetites for information will consistently expand while the corpus of information in the world continues to transform to meet this insatiable demand. In the background, search technology, whether the dominant players of today or future entrants, will continue to improve its ability to match users with what they seek. In between this harmonious sandwich of supply and demand sits SEO. With a Product strategy, we are poised to sit in this sweet spot and weather the winds of the future easily.

Stay flexible. Be more attached to strategy than tactics. There is always an ideal scenario, but then, there is reality. With a flexible playbook, you should be able to adapt to any situation thrown at you and succeed beyond your wildest dreams.

When in doubt, measure, test, and continue to adapt. We know change is coming. It's just a matter of how.

MEASURE

It's hard to learn from data or test assumptions if you don't have good data.

Ensure you first have access to and are consistently looking at the right data. If you don't have Google and Bing Search Consoles set up for your website, that should be on your task list today. Once you have access, they should be your sole sources of reporting on traffic and search visibility. Internal reporting and even Google Analytics have too many inconsistencies in reporting data to be reliable sources of truth on how much organic traffic you have. External SEO tools make broad-based assumptions about visibility using keyword-ranking data, but these are just assumptions. The best data about how you appear in search engines is going to come directly from search engines.

After developing a baseline for how much search traffic you are generating, you want to make sure you measure how you are benefiting from this traffic. Ideally, SEO traffic should be a channel in your overall business KPI reporting, but this could be a challenge for some companies due to the higher-funnel nature of the channel. Knowing where organic traffic fits into the customer journey might mean needing multi-touch attribution, which is certainly not easy to implement. If this is an insurmountable challenge, don't give up. Instead, look for a proxy that shows the SEO traffic is driving top-line results beyond just traffic. (These proxies will be specific to every company, but some common ones are leads filled out, numbers of pages viewed, returning visits, or anything else that shows users progressed toward a conversion event.)

TEST AND OPTIMIZE

SEO is never a one-and-done process. Just because you have seen some success from your efforts doesn't mean it's time to move onto something different. This is precisely when you start to really dig in. The Product strategy and tactics you have implemented up to this point have been uniquely yours and customized for your own situation. After you have developed a flexible and strategic approach, you are going to take your knowledge and make a much bigger investment.

By this point, you will know more about your search user and product-market fit than anyone else in the world. Use this knowledge to improve your product and scale your offering to even more users. Add more features and content based on requests from your customers. Look at Google Search Console to find queries you haven't yet addressed. Test new layouts that may improve conversion.

Don't assume you have unlocked the full potential of your product with just the first version. You have to keep making improvements until there are no more changes to make.

One note on testing and experimentation: most sites cannot do statistically significant A/B testing on SEO. (A/B testing is where you see which of two versions performs better on some predefined metric, but you need a certain population to test on, and that population needs to be representative of the larger population of, say, potential customers. SEO nearly always has a population issue.) Because of this, A/B testing will rarely provide good enough data. However, large sites that are largely templatized (e-commerce sites with thousands of pages, as an example) can make a change on a large number of random pages, and if there is a perceived difference in performance against a control, you can better assume all those unknown variables were accounted for within the test bucket.

Regardless of whether you can achieve the high bar for scientific testing on your site, you should still be constantly testing ideas to see what might unlock more growth. As you observe various levers in your SEO efforts, build a test queue of ideas you can pull from. There should never be an occasion where you don't have some sort of experiment in flight to help learn something new. At a minimum, you can test title tags, content headers, meta descriptions, and content styles to see what has a greater impact on user behavior. What drives results? What drives conversion clicks? What will do more of both?

You should invest heavily in areas specific to your products and business categories. The knowledge you gain on how your business performs in search will be as much an asset and intellectual property as anything in your business and critical to the success of your SEO. Tests should always use a meaningful KPI as a success metric, such as increased revenue. A change might lead to lower average ranking positions on search, but if its net result is higher conversions, it is a winner.

User behavior and search algorithms are always improving, so you should be, too. As an example, I recently experimented with adding the word "free" to title tags on pages that offered a free download. I saw an increase in clicks and subsequent downloads. Given the number of variables, it would be nearly impossible to know how much of a difference my one change made on a handful of pages. Regardless, it appeared to be a positive result without negative implications, so I kept it.

HUMAN-CENTERED SEO LASTS

Ultimately, the beauty of SEO is that while there are rules, best practices, and even playbooks to follow, SEO is truly organic. Users are human. While they might typically operate within known patterns, search demand can be entirely unpredictable. More than one out of every seven searches conducted on Google is brand new!

At the same time, search engine algorithms (from all search engines) utilize AI and machine learning to predict what might be the best results for a query based on what humans need. The specifics of what will rank at what time are locked away in software to be determined only at the moment they are required. Therefore, the best tool you will ever have for SEO is your own mind. Your best chances of success happen when you internalize everything that is known about SEO and season it with the capabilities only humans have. You will go far if you focus on customer empathy, creativity, and human intellect.

SEO is ultimately a task by humans for humans.

CONCLUSION

When small businesses compete directly with big brands online, it is very expensive. Large, well-capitalized businesses dominate paid-marketing chains.

This is where SEO comes in as the savior. While search engines have a clear preference for brands due to user engagement and other signals, users don't necessarily have that preference when there is no visible brand. There are millions and millions of search queries where there is not a recognizable brand in the results. If you are sufficiently creative around Blue Ocean SEO and develop a product-led effort, you will find the utopian greenspace where you will be on a level playing field with the biggest players in the world.

Create a product offering specifically for the search user. If you create the product, there is no competition! Even better, when you use the right inputs to create the product (hint: user data), you will also be generating traffic. Users will inevitably click when you have created something just for them.

To make Product-Led SEO successful, you need to do the hard work of figuring out what to create and making that creation delight the customer. Don't shy away from the hard work just to write content based on what keyword-research tools suggest. Writing content based on content research is exactly what everyone else does, and without an edge over the competition, there is no rational reason why your content would be ranked first. Your best efforts can be eclipsed in a short time. If you make something special and unique, on the other hand, yours will always be the first player (and likely the most important one) in that space, no matter who tries to compete against you.

Put in the time to do Product-Led SEO, and your investment will pay off for many years.

THE TIME IS NOW

Henry Ford famously said, "Pausing advertising to save money is like stopping a clock to save time."

There will always be recessions and excuses not to start a new, unproven SEO effort. Uncertainty is not the time to hit pause. For any company that has not invested in organic marketing, an uncertain time might be the best time to explore if there is an untapped opportunity in SEO.

I want you to look back years from now and say that my book made a difference to you and your business. I want you to apply these principles in Product-Led SEO and from them gain unprecedented—even miraculous—growth. But to do so will take consistent, strategic effort.

The time to begin is now.

WHAT WE HAVE LEARNED

We started this book by discussing what is and is not SEO. Contrary to what many people believe, SEO is not an effort to manipulate users and search engines. SEO, done properly, optimizes for the realities of how search engines work and people search. Websites can certainly get by without ever doing SEO, and many choose to do so, but why would you leave such an important and valuable channel to chance?

In Chapter One, we discussed how search engines work. Search engines want to satisfy a user's curiosity and need for information in the fastest and most efficient way possible. This means they run algorithms—which are a series of conditional rules in computer code—to both understand the intent of a user's query and the meaning of a piece of content (text, image, video, and, eventually, audio). Nowhere in a search engine's set of goals is there a target of sending traffic to websites. Every part of its mission is around satisfying a user's needs.

As a result, trying to fool the algorithms is a losing game. Far better for a website to keep its focus on the end goal of satisfying a user's needs. If it does, it may be impacted by algorithm updates but likely in a positive way as lesser-quality webpages are removed from the index. At times, there could be negative impacts, and that's fine, too. Serving users will always turn out better in the long run.

In Chapter Two, we introduced the idea of Product-Led SEO. The Product-Led SEO approach rejects the idea of using keyword research and search insights to build an SEO effort. Instead, SEO traffic should come from building a specific content offering designed to draw in search users.

There is always a need for more answers on every topic online.

You should create those answers with something new and not just copy whatever has been done by others. The most successful Product-Led SEO efforts will take advantage of content that merges many different data sources into one offering in a programmatic manner and has an extremely high limit of possible iterations that you could create.

You might be able to use software to give you ideas or updates about your SEO positioning, but you cannot build SEO with software alone.

In Chapter Three, we discuss the importance of doing SEO for humans, by humans. Knowing what to hire for is just as important as knowing who to hire.

In Chapter Four, we really dug deep into how SEO should not be viewed as its own channel with its own metrics but instead as a part of the digital-marketing process. For many businesses, SEO will be at the top of the funnel, where users who are just exploring options will discover your business. Once they have found you, it becomes the job of the other marketing channels— paid, social, email, and offline—to bring those users closer to a conversion event.

Reporting and measuring SEO will only get more complex as the world of technology becomes more diverse, as we discussed in Chapter Five. An ideal Product-Led SEO effort will be built in a Blue Ocean, which is the white space where no competitor has thought to develop a product offering.

Chapter Six is the only part of this book where we dug into the tactics that dozens of other books and hundreds of blogs have devoted their pages to. Once you have a strategic direction, you will know how to deploy tactics. The recommendation has always been to create high-quality content that uses the words people search, create an easily understood website, and get people to link to it.

In Chapter Seven, we carried our lessons about how to execute on Product-Led SEO into real-world practice. Knowing the potential user of your product means also having an understanding of their search nuances and platforms and the location and culture from which they're searching. Optimize for YOUR user, don't just fulfill SEO best practices as if they were items on a checklist.

There will always be changes in where, how, and when people search, but with a Product-Led SEO approach, you should always be adapting to users and not just chasing the next new thing.

In Chapter Eight, we discussed how to implement these ideas in an enterprise. The rules for SEO are the same for all companies in all categories and of all sizes. In small sites and companies, SEO success hinges on executing best practices; however, within large enterprises, SEO success rides on the ability of the functional leaders to bring others along with their vision.

The same minor change that could be done in minutes on a small website could take months in a large enterprise where many different teams need to have their say. Within enterprises, there are also defined rules for how initiatives need to be planned, prioritized, and resourced. Working within the confines of these rules is essential.

Finally, in our last chapter, we talked about how to run a

Product-Led SEO effort, from building a multi-disciplinary team or collaboration to convincing others. We highlighted the importance of staying flexible and continuing to test and optimize as you grow. If there is any constant in life and SEO, it is change.

THE POTENTIAL

Product-Led SEO will open up a brand-new acquisition channel for you that can and will bring significant results if you put in the work. However, don't get too comfortable. Whatever you do, success will quickly slip away if you stop paying attention to SEO as a channel. Stay on top of your metrics, keep an eye on the competition, and, most importantly, never lose sight of the user.

My hope is that as you read about Product-Led SEO, it will guide you to take action for what is best for your company. It is easy to continue growing paid-marketing campaigns if they are currently working for you, but that may not always be the case, and when you stop, your results stop. Paid marketing is like renting a house: you never build any equity. SEO is like owning a house: you may have a big mortgage, but every month you earn a little bit more equity in your home. Investing in good SEO practices always pays off in the long run; you just need to have the patience to see it all the way through.

YOU MUST DO THE WORK

In my fifteen years of being deeply involved in SEO, I have heard many declarations around why an SEO effort ultimately ended up not being as successful as hoped, but I have found only one explanation to be factual. Most SEO efforts I have seen fail did so simply because of a lack of execution. There were plans and plans of plans, but somehow, none of it was ever implemented. The best-laid strategies went to waste because no one bothered to take the first step.

I once worked with a company for an entire year, and they somehow managed to not make a single SEO change during that period. At the end of the year, they wrote off SEO as a channel that was never going to work for them. In that, they were absolutely correct: SEO was not going to work for them if they would not try. Changing title tags, improving page speed, and even writing a handful of keyword-targeted blog posts are not what I would ever consider to be building SEO. Developing a strategy to reach a total addressable online market with scaled content is a true SEO effort.

In stark contrast, I had the opportunity to work with a company that had thousands of employees and the trappings of bureaucracy that typically accompany companies of that size, and I expected every little change to be akin to moving skyscrapers. In truth, change was hard, as there were many layers of approval required, but they were willing to move those buildings. Designs had to be approved by multiple parties and even Legal teams. Keyword choices had to be checked by internal teams and even external agencies.

In mere weeks, they accomplished what even smaller companies would find challenging to complete in that timeframe. Their belief in the benefits of this channel drove them to do the impossible. They achieved exactly what they had hoped for. By building a Product-Led SEO approach, they unlocked their opportunities and developed a new search category online that will drive revenue long into the future.

YOUR CHOICE

It is your choice—who would you like to be? The do-nothing company that failed before they even started, or the company that pushed through a strategy and reaped the rewards? Whether you succeed or fail is up to you. Economic downturns, search engine algorithm updates, personality conflicts, and manipulative competitors can be excuses for why you can't succeed or simply obstacles to maneuver around. Change your mindset and choose the latter.

My closing advice to you is as follows: I strongly believe Product-Led SEO is an ideal that will help most companies be successful at SEO, but don't overthink it. It is far better for you to try something small than to come up with the best Product-Led SEO strategy that never gets implemented. If you are to succeed in SEO, you just need to do something. Small successes will inspire people to join your efforts and lead to bigger wins. Now, go out there and do it before someone else beats you to it!

I would love to hear from you on how this book and the ideas I put forward in it might have helped you. Please find me on LinkedIn, send me an email at eli@productledseo.com, *or check out the home-page for this book at productledseo.com.*

My best to you.

Eli Schwartz

ACKNOWLEDGMENTS

I am eternally grateful to all the people who have helped shape my career and the people who supported me in writing this book. First and foremost are the managers I have been privileged to work for and who pushed me to be the best I could be. Hesky Kutscher, Matt Heist, Gallant Chen, Ada Chen Rekhi, Luis Franco, Steve Norall, Selina Tobaccowala, Tom Hale, and Leela Srinivasan. While I learned a great deal from my managers, I gained even more from the people I was privileged to manage. A special thank you to my SurveyMonkey team: Stewart Mohammadi, Bill Shaw, Ivan Beitsayad, and Carla Rucian.

I am so grateful for all the friends and colleagues I have been privileged to work with, but there are two people who deserve specific thanks. John Rampton, who pushed me to begin writing on search blogs while he was the Managing Editor at Search Engine Journal, and Kevin Hale, who introduced me to some amazing Y Combinator companies where I was able to help shape their SEO growth.

Thank you to Adam Grant, Jay Baer, Joe Pulizzi, and Chris Yeh for motivating me to write this book.

Thank you to all the people who helped make this book a reality by proofreading, suggesting edits, and driving it to completion: Alex Hughes Capell, Deanna Rampton, Jake Gronsky, Bill Shaw, Stewart Mohammadi, Michael Bonfils, and Marty Weintraub.

Thank you to Abe Karmel for the headshots.

Thank you to my parents, George and Chava Schwartz, for their unconditional love and support.

Finally, I never could have done this without the support of my wife, Shona, who was the first published author in my family, and my children, Gavriel, Ariel, Ilan, and Daniel.

ABOUT THE AUTHOR

ELI SCHWARTZ is an SEO expert and consultant with more than a decade of experience working for leading B2B and B2C companies. Eli's strategies have generated millions of dollars in revenue for some of the internet's top websites. He has helped clients like Shutterstock, WordPress, Blue Nile, Quora, and Zendesk execute highly successful global SEO strategies.

As head of SurveyMonkey's SEO team, Eli oversaw the company's global operations, helped launch the first Asia-Pacific office, and grew the company's organic search from just 1 percent of revenue to a key driver of global revenue. Eli's work has been featured by *TechCrunch*, Entrepreneur.com, and Y Combinator, and he has given talks at business schools and keynoted conferences around the world.

Printed in Great Britain
by Amazon

11845166R00150